CELTIC
MYTHS & LEGENDS

❋   ❋   ❋

First published in Great Britain by Brockhampton Press, a member of the Hodder Headline Group,
20 Bloomsbury Street, London WC1B 3QA.

Copyright © 1998 Brockhampton Press.

ISBN 1 86019 212 2

A copy of the CIP data is available from the British Library upon request.

Created and produced by Flame Tree Publishing, a part of The Foundry Creative Media Company Limited,
The Long House, Antrobus Road, Chiswick, London W4 5HY.

CELTIC
Myths & Legends

O. B. DUANE

CONTENTS

INTRODUCTION

HE ATTEMPT TO ASSIGN a precise date to the birth of Celtic civilization has proved a complicated and problematic task, leading to many differences of opinion among historians and archaeologists. A straightforward answer to this and a number of other questions arising from the study of Celtic culture is rendered almost impossible by the fact that the Celts cannot simply be catalogued as a geographically unified race. Their evolution, unlike that of the Romans, is not well documented, nor is there any evidence of an organized ancient civic structure which might reveal to us more information about these people.

What we do know however, largely as a result of archaeological research, is that the Celts were an extremely imaginative and accomplished race and certainly no other barbarian tribe before them had ever made such a significant contribution to European culture as a whole. Although the Celts were nomads who began life as simple tribesmen scattered across the Alps of northern Europe and along the Upper Danube river, they possessed a fierce conquering spirit which enabled them to dominate Mediterranean society from about 500 BC right up until the Roman Empire began to take shape, roughly in the mid-third century BC. During this era of supremacy, the Celts sacked Rome and Delphi and spread in substantial numbers throughout France, Belgium, Switzerland, the Balkans and Asia Minor. Yet they never managed to establish permanent kingdoms in any of the lands they conquered, nor did they display any aptitude for cultivating a centrally co-ordinated military strategy. The loyalties of the Celts remained tribal rather than imperial and it was surely as a direct consequence of this that by the middle of the first century AD, the Romans occupied most of the old Celtic strongholds of Europe and managed to drive the Celts westwards into Scotland and Ireland.

We are not certain when it was precisely that the Celts arrived in Ireland. Some historians have suggested that the first Celtic immigrants to the British Isles may have arrived as early as the late Bronze Age, in the sixth century BC, but the majority of opinion adheres to the view that the Celts were more firmly established in Ireland during the Iron Age which began around 500 BC. The great stone fort of Dun Aengus on the Aran island of Innismore is positive evidence of the presence

Opposite: As soon as they had learned to write, the Celts began to transcribe for posterity native tales of their pagan lifestyles handed down over countless generations.

of early Celtic barbarians in Ireland whom the natives described as Fir Bolg.

Ireland, unlike other European countries, was never invaded by the Romans and it therefore escaped the systematic oppression of native language and traditions Rome insisted upon. Ireland's culture as a result remained largely unchanged up until the spread of Christianity, in contrast to its neighbour Britain, which by the year AD 40 had completely succumbed to Roman authority. An indigenous Celtic civilization was preserved in Ireland and ancient traditions were allowed to flourish. The spectacular array of Celtic artefacts discovered in various locations throughout Europe, including jewellery, pottery, decorated weapons, stone carvings, High Crosses and stunning illuminated manuscripts, has left us in little doubt that the Celts were extremely gifted craftsmen, but Ireland, unique among other countries penetrated by this race, may boast an additional treasure to add to the vast hoard Celtic culture has bequeathed us. Ireland's ancient literature is unparalleled by any other western European literature of the early Middle Ages in its originality, historical insight, imaginative charm, and sheer lyrical beauty.

The earliest form of narrative the Celts indulged in was no doubt in the oral tradition and we know from later written descriptions of them that storytelling was a favourite pastime and that their men of poetry were highly esteemed figures. Of those nations remaining beyond the influence of Rome, Ireland's was one of the few ancient societies that learned to write. This unusual situation came about as a result of Christian missionary activity, instigated by the Romans, which became widespread throughout the country by the late fifth century. In the fullness of time, the Celts were Christianized, but to begin with, as soon as they had mastered the art of writing, they began to transcribe for posterity native tales in their own vernacular which embodied pre-Christian traditions of their pagan lifestyles handed down over countless generations.

The earliest Irish literary manuscripts now in existence are thought to have been copied from texts written down by the Celts as early as the seventh century, or possibly even earlier. Many of the original

Opposite: Peopled by Queens, gods, noble warriors, fairy women, druids and goblins, Celtic mythology is unparalleled by any other western European literature of the early Middle Ages.

manuscripts were destroyed however, during the Viking raids of the ninth and tenth centuries and only a very few fragmentary texts have survived which were written before AD 1000. Modern organization of Ireland's ancient tales based on these manuscripts divides them into four main groups, or cycles – the Invasions Cycle, the Ulster Cycle, the Fenian Cycle and the Historical Cycle. This volume presents typical

examples of the first three cycles, generally considered to be the most important.

The *Book of Invasions* (*Lebor Gábala*) is a twelfth-century manuscript in which historical and mythical elements are very obviously fused. We discover, for example, that Ireland has been subject to at least six different invasions during the pre-Christian, pagan era, each account documented in an authentic tone and style which, for all that, conflicts with the fairytale physical descriptions of a great many of the invaders and the impossible feats they achieve. Out of this mingled context emerges a group of very powerful and lyrical tales forming the Invasions Cycle which manifests the same constant tension between a reality and a fantasy world. What is reinforced, however, is the Celtic love and worship of natural objects such as rivers and trees and the Celtic belief in a fairy realm, or Otherworld. Central to these stories is a supernatural and highly significant race of people known as the Tuatha De Danann of which more is revealed in the chapters to follow.

The Ulster Cycle is set in the reign of Conchobar mac Nessa and the notorious Queen Medb of Connacht in the first century of the Christian era. The stories are preserved in various manuscripts which date from the twelfth to the fifteenth centuries and are more readily 'historical' in that they are less fanciful, moving towards a firmer exploration of a Celtic society displaying a more elaborate system of law and order. The task of separating fact from fiction is still a difficult one in these tales, but many eminent scholars are agreed that characters such as Cuchulainn, Medb and Conchobar mac Nessa really did exist, however much their exploits and personalities are exaggerated and enhanced by the storytellers. Most of the tales of the Ulster Cycle, including The Birth of Cuchulainn, The Intoxication of the Ulstermen and The Cattle Raid of Cooley are found in their most original form in *The Book of the Dun Cow* (*Lebor na Huidre*) which was written sometime around AD 1100. The book containing 134 folio pages is now housed in the Royal Irish Academy in Dublin.

The earliest tales of the Fenian, or Ossianic cycle, set in the third century of the Christian era during the reign of Conn Céadchathach and his grandson Cormac mac Art, are preserved in manuscripts of the eleventh and twelfth centuries but were almost certainly written several hundreds of years earlier, probably in the eighth century. The Fianna, who are portrayed in these stories as a highly skilled band of volunteer soldiers led by Finn mac Cumaill, have been one of the most popular subjects of

Irish and also Scottish literature since the Celts first immortalized them. The tale of Finn's son Oisín in the Land of Youth belongs less to the heroic tradition of the original Fenian tales, however. The dialogue sequence between Oisín and St Patrick which appeared in the late twelfth century manuscript *The Colloquy of Old Men* (*Agallamh na Seanórach*) is the work of a Christianized storyteller who uses the character and the cycle's narrative framework as a vehicle to introduce a topical Christian theme. This practice of adding additional tales to the cycle was one which continued well into the eighteenth century.

The Historical Cycle, which unfortunately cannot be covered in a volume of this length, includes a colourful multitude of miscellaneous tales and legends including tales of Cormac mac Art, and later kings of ancient Ireland.

⁕   ⁕   ⁕

AUTHOR'S NOTE
The stories gathered in this book are only a selection of the classic myths and legends of Ireland's ancient past. They have been vividly retold with the aim of both inspiring the novice and the enthusiast to delve further into Ireland's glorious tradition of storytelling. A short pronunciation guide and glossary are included at the back of this volume to add to the reader's enjoyment.

THE INVASIONS CYCLE
TALES OF THE TUATHA DE DANANN
AND THE EARLY MILESIANS

 he three stories which introduce this volume are based on tales selected from the *Book of Invasions*, otherwise known as the Mythological Cycle. This chapter begins after the conquest of the Fir Bolg by the Tuatha De Danann, the god-like race, whose name translates as 'the people of the god whose mother is Dana'. Three of the most outstanding stories have been chosen for this section, each of which has an especially powerful narrative impact.

The Tuatha De Danann are recorded as having originally travelled to Erin from the northern islands of Greece around 2000 BC. They possessed great gifts of magic and druidism and they ruled the country until their defeat by the Milesians, when they were forced to establish an underground kingdom known as the Otherworld or the Sidhe, meaning Hollow Hills.

Lugh[1] of the Long Arm, who also appears later in the Ulster Cycle as Cuchulainn's divine father, emerges as one of the principal heroes of the Tuatha De Danann who rescues his people from the tyranny of the Fomorians. The Quest of the Children of Tuirenn, together with the sorrowful account of Lir's children, are undoubtedly two of the great epic tales of this cycle.

The Wooing of Etain which concludes the trio, was probably written sometime in the eighth century. The story unfolds after the People of Dana are dispossessed by the Children of Miled and for the first time the notion of a Land of Youth, or Otherworld, is introduced, a theme again returned to in the third and final Fenian Cycle.

[1] Pronounced Lu, *gh* is silent, as in English.

The Quest of the Children of Tuirenn

NUADA OF THE SILVER HAND rose to become King of the Tuatha De Danann during the most savage days of the early invasions. The Fomorians, a repulsive band of sea-pirates, were the fiercest of opponents who swept through the country destroying cattle and property and imposing tribute on the people of the land. Every man of the Tuatha De Danann, no matter how rich or poor, was required to pay one ounce of gold to the Fomorians and those who neglected to pay this tax at the annual assembly on the Hill of Uisneach were maimed or murdered without compassion. Balor of the Evil Eye was leader of these brutal invaders, and it was well known that when he turned his one glaring eyeball on his foes they immediately fell dead as if struck by a thunderbolt. Everyone lived in mortal fear of Balor, for no weapon had yet been discovered that could slay or even injure him. Times were bleak for the Tuatha De Danann and the people had little faith in King Nuada who appeared powerless to resist Balor's tyranny and oppression. As the days passed by, they yearned for a courageous leader who would rescue them from their life of wretched servitude.

The appalling misery of the Tuatha De Danann became known far and wide and, after a time, it reached the ears of Lugh of the Long Arm of the fairymounds, whose father was Cian, son of Cainte. As soon as he had grown to manhood, Lugh had proven his reputation as one of the most fearless warriors and was so revered by the elders of Fairyland that they had placed in his charge the wondrous magical gifts of Manannan the sea-god which had protected their people for countless generations. Lugh rode the magnificent white steed of Manannan, known as Aenbarr, a horse as fleet of foot as the wailing gusts of winter whose charm was such that no rider was ever wounded while seated astride her. He had the boat of Manannan, which could read a man's thoughts and travel in whatever direction its keeper demanded. He also wore Manannan's breast-plate and body armour which no weapon could ever pierce, and he carried the mighty sword known as 'The Retaliator' that could cut through any battle shield.

Opposite:
The Fomorians were the fiercest of opponents who swept through the country destroying cattle and property and imposing tribute on the people of the land.

The day approached once more for the People of Dana to pay their annual taxes to the Fomorians and they gathered together, as was customary, on the Hill of Uisneach to await the arrival of Balor's men. As they stood fearful and terrified in the chill morning air, several among them noticed a strange cavalry coming over the plain from the east towards them. At the head of this impressive group,

seated high in command above the rest, was Lugh of the Long Arm, whose proud and noble countenance mirrored the splendour of the rising sun. The King was summoned to witness the spectacle and he rode forth to salute the leader of the strange army. The two had just begun to converse amiably when they were interrupted by the approach of a grimy-looking band of men, instantly known to all as Fomorian tax-collectors. King Nuada bowed respectfully towards them and instructed his subjects to deliver their tributes without delay. Such a sad sight angered and humiliated Lugh of the Long Arm and he drew the King aside and began to reproach him:

'Why do your subjects bow before such an evil-eyed brood,' he demanded, 'when they do not show you any mark of respect in return?'

'We are obliged to do this,' replied Nuada. 'If we refuse we would be killed instantly and our land has witnessed more than enough bloodshed at the hands of the Fomorians.'

'Then it is time for the Tuatha De Danann to avenge this great injustice,' replied Lugh, and with that, he began slaughtering Balor's emissaries single-handedly until all but one lay dead at his feet. Dragging the surviving creature before him, Lugh ordered him to deliver a stern warning to Balor:

'Return to your leader,' he thundered, 'and inform him that he no longer has any power over the People of Dana. Lugh of the Long Arm, the greatest of warriors, is more than eager to enter into combat with him if he possesses enough courage to meet the challenge.'

Knowing that these words would not fail to enrage Balor, Lugh lost little time preparing himself for battle. He enlisted the King's help in assembling the strongest men in the kingdom to add to his own powerful army. Shining new weapons of steel were provided and three thousand of the swiftest white horses were made ready for his men. A magnificent fleet of ships, designed to withstand the most venomous ocean waves, remained moored at port, awaiting the moment when Balor and his malicious crew would appear on the horizon.

The time finally arrived when the King received word that Balor's fierce army had landed at Eas Dara on the northwest coast of Connacht. Within hours, the Fomorians had pillaged the lands of Bodb the Red and plundered the homes of noblemen throughout the province. Hearing of this wanton destruction, Lugh of the Long Arm was more determined than ever to secure victory for the Tuatha De Danann. He rode across the plains of Erin back to his home to enlist the help of Cian, his father, who controlled all the armies of the fairymounds. His two

Opposite:
Everyone lived in mortal fear of Balor, for no weapon had yet been discovered that could slay or even injure him.

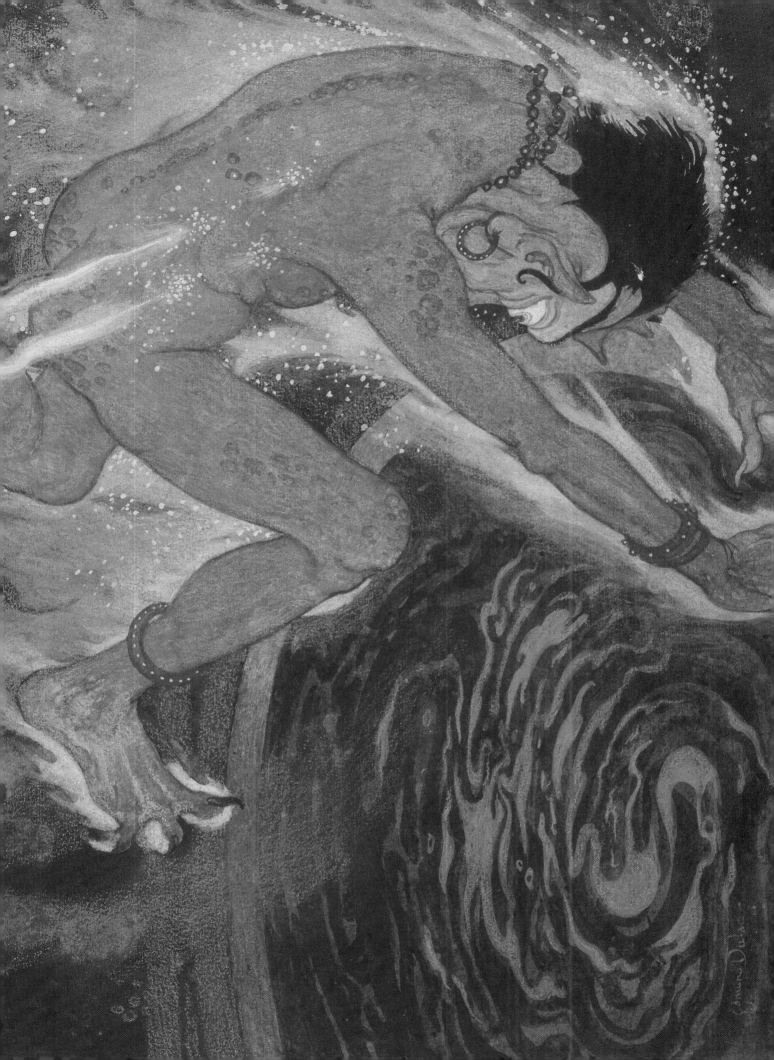

uncles, Cu and Cethen, also offered their support and the three brothers set off in different directions to round up the remaining warriors of Fairyland.

Cian journeyed northwards and he did not rest until he reached Mag Muirthemne on the outskirts of Dundalk. As he crossed the plain, he observed three men, armed and mailed, riding towards him. At first he did not recognize them, but as they drew closer, he knew them to be the sons of Tuirenn whose names were Brian, Iucharba and Iuchar. A long-standing feud had existed for years between the sons of Cainte and the sons of Tuirenn and the hatred and enmity they felt towards each other was certain to provoke a deadly contest. Wishing to avoid an unequal clash of arms, Cian glanced around him for a place to hide and noticed a large herd of swine grazing nearby. He struck himself with a druidic wand and changed himself into a pig. Then he trotted off to join the herd and began to root up the ground like the rest of them.

The sons of Tuirenn were not slow to notice that the warrior who had been riding towards them had suddenly vanished into thin air. At first, they all appeared puzzled by his disappearance, but then Brian, the eldest of the three, began to question his younger brothers knowingly:

'Surely brothers you also saw the warrior on horseback,' he said to them. 'Have you no idea what became of him?'

'We do not know,' they replied.

'Then you are not fit to call yourselves warriors,' chided Brian, 'for that horseman can be no friend of ours if he is cowardly enough to change himself into one of these swine. The instruction you received in the City of Learning has been wasted on you if you cannot even tell an enchanted beast from a natural one.'

And as he was saying this, he struck Iucharba and Iuchar with his own druidic wand, transforming them into two sprightly hounds that howled and yelped impatiently to follow the trail of the enchanted pig.

Before long, the pig had been hunted down and driven into a small wood where Brian cast his spear at it, driving it clean through the animal's chest. Screaming in pain, the injured pig began to speak in a human voice and begged his captors for mercy:

'Allow me a dignified death,' the animal pleaded. 'I am originally a human being, so grant me permission to pass into my own shape before I die.'

'I will allow this,' answered Brian, 'since I am often less reluctant to kill a man than a pig.'

Opposite:
Cian, son of Cainte, readily agreed to help his son gather the armies of the fairymounds for the great war against Balor.

Then Cian, son of Cainte, stood before them with blood trickling down his cloak from the gaping wound in his chest.

'I have outwitted you,' he cried, 'for if you had killed me as a pig you would only be sentenced for killing an animal, but now you must kill me in my own human shape. And I must warn you that the penalty you will pay for this crime is far greater than any ever paid before on the death of a nobleman, for the weapons you shall use will cry out in anguish, proclaiming your wicked deed to my son, Lugh of the Long Arm'.

'We will not slay you with any weapons in that case,' replied Brian triumphantly, 'but with the stones that lie on the ground around us.' And the three brothers began to pelt Cian with jagged rocks and stones until his body was a mass of wounds and he fell to the earth battered and lifeless. The sons of Tuirenn then buried him where he had fallen in an unmarked grave and hurried off to join the war against the Fomorians.

With the great armies of Fairyland and the noble cavalcade of King Nuada at his side, Lugh of the Long Arm won battle after battle against Balor and his men. Spears shot savagely through the air and scabbards clashed furiously until at last, the Fomorians could hold out no longer. Retreating to the coast, the terrified survivors and their leader boarded their vessels and sailed as fast as the winds could carry them back through the northern mists towards their own depraved land. Lugh of the Long Arm became the hero of his people and they presented him with the finest trophies of valour the kingdom had to offer, including a golden war chariot, studded with precious jewels which was driven by four of the brawniest milk-white steeds.

When the festivities had died down somewhat, and the Tuatha De Danann had begun to lead normal lives once more, Lugh began to grow anxious for news of his father. He called several of his companions to him and appealed to them for information, but none among them had received tidings of Cian since the morning he had set off towards the north to muster the armies of the fairymounds.

'I know that he is no longer alive,' said Lugh, 'and I give you my word that I will not rest again, or allow food or drink to pass my lips, until I have knowledge of what happened to him.'

Opposite: Lugh of the Long Arm had an enchanted childhood in Fairyland and grew to become a brave and noble warrior - a hero to his people.

And so Lugh, together with a number of his kinsmen, rode forth to the place where he and his father had parted company. From here, the horse of Manannan guided him to the Plain of Muirthemne where Cian had met his tragic death. As soon as he entered the shaded wood, the stones of the ground began to cry out in despair and they told Lugh of how the sons of Tuirenn had murdered his father and buried him in the earth. Lugh wept bitterly when he heard this tale and implored his men to help him dig up the grave so that he might discover in what cruel manner Cian had been slain. The body was raised from the ground and the litter of wounds on his father's cold flesh was revealed to him. Lugh rose gravely to his feet and swore angry vengeance on the sons of Tuirenn:

'This death has so exhausted my spirit that I cannot hear through my ears, and I cannot see anything with my eyes, and there is not one pulse beating in my heart for grief of my father. Sorrow and destruction will fall on those that committed this crime and they shall suffer long when they are brought to justice.'

The body was returned to the ground and Lugh carved a headstone and placed it on the grave. Then, after a long period of mournful silence, he mounted his horse and headed back towards Tara where the last of the victory celebrations were taking place at the palace.

Lugh of the Long Arm sat calmly and nobly next to King Nuada at the banqueting table and looked around him until he caught sight of the three sons of Tuirenn. As soon as he had fixed his eye on them, he stood up and ordered the Chain of Attention of the Court to be shaken so that everyone present would fall silent and listen to what he had to say.

'I put to you all a question,' said Lugh. 'I ask each of you what punishment you would inflict upon the man that had murdered your father?'

The King and his warriors were astonished at these words, but finally Nuada spoke up and enquired whether it was Lugh's own father that had been killed.

'It is indeed my own father who lies slain,' replied Lugh 'and I see before me in this very room the men who carried out the foul deed.'

'Then it would be far too lenient a punishment to strike them down directly,' said the King. 'I myself would ensure that they died a lingering death and I would cut off a single limb each day until they fell down before me writhing in agony'

Those who were assembled agreed with the King's verdict and even the sons of Tuirenn nodded their heads in approval. But Lugh declared that he did not wish to kill any of the Tuatha De Danann, since they were his own people. Instead, he would insist that the perpetrators pay a heavy fine, and as he spoke he stared accusingly towards Brian, Iuchar and Iucharba, so that the identity of the murderers was clearly exposed to all. Overcome with guilt and shame, the sons of Tuirenn could not bring themselves to deny their crime, but bowed their heads and stood prepared for the sentence Lugh was about to deliver.

'This is what I demand of you,' he announced.

Three ripened apples
The skin of a pig
A pointed spear
Two steeds and a chariot
Seven pigs
A whelping pup
A cooking spit
Three shouts on a hill.

'And,' Lugh added, 'if you think this fine too harsh, I will now reduce part of it. But if you think it acceptable, you must pay it in full, without variation, and pledge your loyalty to me before the royal guests gathered here.'

'We do not think it too great a fine,' said Brian, 'nor would it be too large a compensation if you multiplied it a hundredfold. Therefore, we will go out in search of all these things you have described and remain faithful to you until we have brought back every last one of these objects.'

'Well, now,' said Lugh, 'since you have bound yourselves before the court to the quest assigned you, perhaps you would like to learn more detail of what lies in store,' And he began to elaborate on the tasks that lay before the sons of Tuirenn.

'The apples I have requested of you,' Lugh continued, 'are the three apples of the Hesperides growing in the gardens of the Eastern World. They are the colour of burnished gold and have the power to cure the bloodiest wound or the most horrifying illness. To retrieve these apples, you will need great courage, for the people of the east have been forewarned that three young warriors will one day attempt to deprive them of their most cherished possessions.

'And the pig's skin I have asked you to bring me will not be easy to obtain either, for it belongs to the King of Greece who values it above everything else. It too has the power to heal all wounds and diseases.

'The spear I have demanded of you is the poisoned spear kept by Pisar, King of Persia. This spear is so keen to do battle that its blade must always be kept in a cauldron of freezing water to prevent its fiery heat melting the city in which it is kept.

'And do you know who keeps the chariot and the two steeds I wish to receive from you?' Lugh continued.

'We do not know,' answered the sons of Tuirenn.

'They belong to Dobar, King of Sicily,' said Lugh, 'and such is their unique charm that they are equally happy to ride over sea or land, and the chariot they pull is unrivalled in beauty and strength.

'And the seven pigs you must gather together are the pigs of Asal, King of the Golden Pillars. Every night they are slaughtered, but every morning they are found alive again, and any person who eats part of them is protected from ill-health for the rest of his life.

'Three further things I have demanded of you,' Lugh went on. 'The whelping hound you must bring me guards the palace of the King of Iruad. Failinis is her name and all the wild beasts of the world fall down in terror before her, for she is stronger and more splendid than any other creature known to man.

'The cooking-spit I have called for is housed in the kitchen of the fairywomen on Inis Findcuire, an island surrounded by the most perilous waters that no man has ever safely reached.

'Finally, you must give the three shouts requested of you on the Hill of Midcain where it is prohibited for any man other than the sons of Midcain to cry aloud. It was here that my father received his warrior training and here that his death will be hardest felt. Even if I should one day forgive you of my father's murder, it is certain that the sons of Midcain will not.'

As Lugh finished speaking, the children of Tuirenn were struck dumb by the terrifying prospect of all that had to be achieved by them and they went at once to where their father lived and told him of the dreadful sentence that had been pronounced on them.

'It is indeed a harsh fine,' said Tuirenn, 'but one that must be paid if you are guilty, though it may end tragically for all three of you.' Then he advised his sons to return to Lugh to beg the loan of the boat of Manannan that would carry them swiftly over the seas on their difficult quest. Lugh kindly agreed to give them the boat and they made their way towards the port accompanied by their father. With heavy hearts, they exchanged a sad farewell and wearily set sail on the first of many arduous journeys.

'We shall go in search of the apples to begin with,' said Brian, and his command was answered immediately by the boat of Manannan which steered a course towards the Eastern World and sailed without stopping until it came to rest in a sheltered harbour in the lands of the Hesperides. The brothers then considered how best they might remove the apples from the garden in which they were growing, and it was eventually decided among them that they should transform themselves into three screeching hawks.

'The tree is well guarded,' Brian declared, 'but we shall circle it, carefully avoiding the arrows that will be hurled at us until they have all been spent. Then we will swoop on the apples and carry them off in our beaks.'

The three performed this task without suffering the slightest injury and headed back towards the boat with the stolen fruit. The news of the theft had soon spread throughout the kingdom, however, and the king's three daughters quickly changed themselves into three-taloned ospreys and pursued the hawks over the sea. Shafts of lightning lit up the skies around them and struck the wings of the hawks, scorching their feathers and causing them to plummet towards the waters below. But Brian managed to take hold of his druidic wand and he

Opposite: They dressed themselves appropriately and set their sail for Greece, composing flattering verses in honour of King Tuis.

transformed himself and his brothers into swans that darted below the waves until the ospreys had given up the chase and it was safe for them to return to the boat.

After they had rested awhile, it was decided that they should travel on to Greece in search of the skin of the pig.

'Let us visit this land in the shape of three bards of Erin,' said Brian, 'for if we appear as such, we will be honoured and respected as men of wit and wisdom.'

They dressed themselves appropriately and set sail for Greece composing some flattering verses in honour of King Tuis as they journeyed along. As soon as they had landed, they made their way to the palace and were enthusiastically welcomed as dedicated men of poetry who had travelled far in search of a worthy patron. An evening of drinking and merry-making followed; verses were read aloud by the King's poets and many ballads were sung by the court musicians. At length, Brian rose to his feet and began to recite the poem he had written for King Tuis. The King smiled rapturously to hear himself described as 'the oak among kings' and encouraged Brian to accept some reward for his pleasing composition.

'I will happily accept from you the pig's skin you possess,' said Brian, 'for I have heard that it can cure all wounds.'

'I would not give this most precious object to the finest poet in the world,' replied the King, 'but I shall fill the skin three times over with red gold, one skin for each of you, which you may take away with you as the price of your poem.'

The brothers agreed to this and the King's attendants escorted them to the treasure-house where the gold was to be measured out. They were about to weigh the very last share when Brian suddenly snatched the pig's skin and raced from the room, striking down several of the guards as he ran. He had just found his way to the outer courtyard when King Tuis appeared before him, his sword drawn in readiness to win back his most prized possession. Many bitter blows were exchanged and many deep wounds were inflicted by each man on the other until, at last, Brian dealt the King a fatal stroke and he fell to the ground never to rise again.

Opposite:
The fourth stage of the quest took the brothers to the kingdom of Dobar where they offered their services as brave warriors of Erin.

Armed with the pig's skin that could cure their battle wounds, and the apples that could restore them to health, the sons of Tuirenn grew more confident that they would succeed in their quest. They were determined to move on as quickly as possible to the next task Lugh had set them and instructed the boat of Manannan to take them to the land of Persia, to the court of King Pisar, where they appeared once more in the guise of poets. Here they were also made welcome and were treated with honour and distinction. After a time, Brian was called upon to deliver his poem and, as before, he recited some verses in praise of the King which won the approval of all who were gathered. Again, he was persuaded to accept some small reward for his poem and, on this occasion, he requested the magic spear of Persia. But the King grew very angry at this request and the benevolent attitude he had previously displayed soon turned to open hostility:

'It was most unwise of you to demand my beloved spear as a gift,' bellowed the King, 'the only reward you may expect now is to escape death for having made so insolent a request.'

When Brian heard these words he too was incensed and grabbing one of the three golden apples, he flung it at the King's head, dashing out his brains. Then the three brothers rushed from the court, slaughtering all they encountered along the way, and hurried towards the stables where the spear of Pisar lay resting in a cauldron of water. They quickly seized the spear and headed for the boat of Manannan, shouting out their next destination as they ran, so that the boat made itself ready and turned around in the direction of Sicily and the kingdom of Dobar.

'Let us strike up a friendship with the King,' said Brian, 'by offering him our services as soldiers of Erin.'

And when they arrived at Dobar's court they were well received

and admitted at once to the King's great army where they won the admiration of all as the most valiant defenders of the realm. The brothers remained in the King's service for a month and two weeks, but during all this time they never once caught a glimpse of the two steeds and the chariot Lugh of the Long Arm had spoken of.

'We have waited long enough,' Brian announced impatiently. 'Let us go to the King and inform him that we will quit his service unless he shows us his famous steeds and his chariot.'

So they went before King Dobar who was not pleased to receive news of their departure, for he had grown to rely on the three brave warriors. He immediately sent for his steeds and ordered the chariot to be yoked to them and they were paraded before the sons of Tuirenn. Brian watched carefully as the charioteer drove the steeds around in a circle and as they came towards him a second time he sprung onto the nearest saddle and seized the reins. His two brothers fought a fierce battle against those who tried to prevent them escaping, but it was not long before they were at Brian's side, riding furiously through the palace gates, eager to pursue their fifth quest.

They sailed onwards without incident until they reached the land of King Asal of the Pillars of Gold. But their high spirits were quickly vanquished by the sight of a large army guarding the harbour in anticipation of their arrival. For the fame of the sons of Tuirenn was widespread by this time, and their success in carrying away with them the most coveted treasures of the world was well known to all. King Asal himself now came forward to greet them and demanded to know why they had pillaged the lands of other kings and murdered so many in their travels. Then Brian told King Asal of the sentence Lugh of the Long Arm had pronounced upon them and of the many hardships they had already suffered as a result.

'And what have you come here for?' the King enquired.

'We have come for the seven pigs which Lugh has also demanded as part of that compensation,' answered Brian, 'and it would be far better for all of us if you deliver them to us in good will.'

Opposite: Far across the ocean, in the land of Erin, Lugh made sure that every scrap of news reached his ears concerning the sons of Tuirenn.

When the King heard these words, he took counsel with his people, and it was wisely decided that the seven pigs should be handed over peacefully, without bloodshed. The sons of Tuirenn expressed their gratitude to King Asal and pledged their services to him in all future battles. Then Asal questioned them on their next adventure, and when he discovered that they were journeying onwards to the land

of Iruad in search of a puppy hound, he made the following request of them:

'Take me along with you,' he said 'for my daughter is married to the King of Iruad and I am desperate, for love of her, to persuade him to surrender what you desire of him without a show of arms.'

Brian and his brothers readily agreed to this and the boats were made ready for them to sail together for the land of Iruad.

When they reached the shores of the kingdom, Asal went ahead in search of his son-in-law and told him the tale of the sons of Tuirenn from beginning to end and of how he had rescued his people from a potentially bloody war. But Iruad was not disposed to listen to the King's advice and adamantly refused to give up his hound without a fight. Seizing his weapon, he gave the order for his men to begin their attack and went himself in search of Brian in order to challenge him to single combat. A furious contest ensued between the two and they struck each other viciously and angrily. Eventually, however, Brian succeeded in overpowering King Iruad and he hauled him before Asal, bound and gagged like a criminal.

'I have spared his life,' said Brian, 'perhaps he will now hand over the hound in recognition of my clemency.'

The King was untied and the hound was duly presented to the sons of Tuirenn who were more than pleased that the battle had come to a swift end. And there was no longer any bitterness between Iruad and the three brothers, for Iruad had been honestly defeated and had come to admire his opponents. They bid each other a friendly farewell and the sons of Tuirenn took their leave of the land of the Golden Pillars and set out to sea once again.

Far across the ocean in the land of Erin, Lugh of the Long Arm had made certain that news of every success achieved by the sons of Tuirenn had been brought to his attention. He was fully aware that the quest he had set them was almost drawing to a close and became increasingly anxious at the thought. But he desired above everything else to take possession of the valuable objects that had already been recovered, for Balor of the Evil Eye had again reared his ugly head and the threat of another Fomorian invasion was imminent. Seeking to lure the sons of Tuirenn back to Erin, Lugh sent a druidical spell after the brothers, causing them to forget that their sentence had not yet been fully completed. Under its influence, the sons of Tuirenn entertained visions of the heroic

Opposite:
The beautiful land of King Asal of the Pillars of Gold was as enchanting as the Fairyland and lifted the spirits of the three brothers.

reception that awaited them on the shores of the Boyne and their hearts were filled with joy to think that they would soon be reunited with their father.

Within days, their feet had touched on Erin's soil again and they hastened to Tara to the Annual Assembly, presided over by the High King of Erin. Here, they were heartily welcomed by the royal family and the Tuatha De Danann who rejoiced alongside them and praised them for their great courage and valour. And it was agreed that they should submit the tokens of their quest to the High King himself who undertook to examine them and to inform Lugh of the triumphant return of the sons of Tuirenn. A messenger was despatched to Lugh's household and within an hour he had arrived at the palace of Tara, anxious to confront the men he still regarded as his enemies.

'We have paid the fine on your father's life,' said Brian, as he pointed towards the array of objects awaiting Lugh's inspection.

'This is indeed an impressive sight,' replied Lugh of the Long Arm, 'and would suffice as payment for any other murder. But you bound yourselves before the court to deliver everything asked for and I see that you have not done so. Where is the cooking-spit I was promised? And what is to be done about the three shouts on the hill which you have not yet given?'

When the sons of Tuirenn heard this, they realized that they had been deceived and they collapsed exhausted to the floor. Gloom and despair fell upon them as they faced once more the reality of long years of searching and wandering. Leaving behind the treasures that had hitherto protected them, they made their way wearily towards their ship which carried them swiftly away over the storm-tossed seas.

They had spent three months at sea and still they could not discover the smallest trace of the island known as Inis Findcurie. But when their hopes had almost faded, Brian suggested that they make one final search beneath the ocean waves and he put on his magical water-dress and dived over the side of the boat. After two long weeks of swimming in the salt water, he at last happened upon the island, tucked away in a dark hollow of the ocean bed. He immediately went in search of the court and found it occupied by a large group of women, their heads bent in concentration, as they each embroidered a cloth of gold. The women appeared not to notice Brian and he seized this opportunity to move forward to where the cooking-spit rested in a corner of the room. He had just lifted it from the hearth when the women broke into peals of laughter and they laughed long and heartily until finally the eldest of them condescended to address him:

'Take the spit with you, as a reward for your heroism,' she said mockingly, 'but even if your two brothers had attended you here, the weakest of us would have had little trouble preventing you from removing what you came for.'

And Brian took his leave of them knowing they had succeeded in humiliating him, yet he was grateful, nonetheless, that only one task remained to be completed.

They lost no time in directing the boat of Manannan towards their final destination and had reached the Hill of Midcain shortly afterwards, on whose summit they had pledged themselves to give three shouts. But as soon as they had begun to ascend to the top, the guardian of the hill, none other than Midcain himself, came forward to challenge the sons of Tuirenn:

'What is your business in my territory,' demanded Midcain.

'We have come to give three shouts on this hill,' said Brian, 'in fulfilment of the quest we have been forced to pursue in the name of Lugh of the Long Arm.'

'I knew his father well,' replied Midcain, 'and I am under oath not to permit anyone to cry aloud on my hill.'

'Then we have no option but to fight for that permission,' declared Brian, and he rushed at his opponent with his sword before Midcain had the opportunity to draw his own, killing him with a single thrust of his blade through the heart.

Then the three sons of Midcain came out to fight the sons of Tuirenn and the conflict that followed was one of the bitterest and bloodiest ever before fought by any group of warriors. They battled with the strength of wild bears and the ruthlessness of starving lions until they had carved each other to pieces and the grass beneath their feet ran crimson with blood. In the end, however, it was the sons of Tuirenn who were victorious, but their wounds were so deep that they fell to the ground one after the other and waited forlornly for death to come, wishing in vain that they still had the pig skin to cure them.

They had rested a long time before Brian had the strength to speak, and he reminded his brothers that they had not yet given the three shouts on the Hill of Midcain that Lugh had demanded of them. Then slowly they raised themselves up off the ground and did as they had been requested, satisfied at last that they had entirely fulfilled their quest. And after this, Brian lifted his wounded brothers into the boat, promising them a final glimpse of Erin if they would only struggle against death a brief while longer.

And on this occasion the boat of Manannan did not come to a halt on the shores of the Boyne, but moved speedily overland until it reached Dun Tuirenn where the dying brothers were delivered into their father's care. Then Brian, who knew that the end of his life was fast approaching, pleaded fretfully with Tuirenn:

'Go, beloved father,' he urged, 'and deliver this cooking-spit to Lugh, informing him that we have completed all the tasks assigned us. And beg him to allow us to cure our wounds with the pig skin he possesses, for we have suffered long and hard in the struggle to pay the fine on Cian's murder.'

Then Tuirenn rode towards Tara in all haste, fearful that his sons might pass away before his return. And he demanded an audience with Lugh of the Long Arm who came out to meet him at once and graciously received the cooking-spit presented to him.

'My sons are gravely ill and close to death,' Tuirenn exclaimed piteously. 'I beg you to part with the healing pig skin they brought you for one single night, so that I may place it upon their battle wounds and witness it restore them to full health.'

But Lugh of the Long Arm fell silent at this request and stared coldly into the distance towards the Plain of Muirthemne where his father had fallen. When at length he was ready to give Tuirenn his answer, the expression he wore was cruel and menacing and the tone of his voice was severe and merciless:

'I would rather give you the expanse of the earth in gold,' said Lugh, 'than hand over any object that would save the lives of your sons. Let them die in the knowledge that they have achieved something good because of me, and let them thank me for bringing them renown and glory through such a valorous death.'

On hearing these words, Tuirenn hung his head in defeat and accepted that it was useless to bargain with Lugh of the Long Arm. He made his way back despondently to where his sons lay dying and gave them his sad news. The brothers were overcome with grief and despair and were so utterly devastated by Lugh's decision that not one of them lived to see the sun set in the evening sky. Tuirenn's heart was broken in two and after he had placed the last of his sons in the earth, all life departed from him and he fell dead over the bodies of Brian, Iucharba and Iuchar. The Tuatha De Danann witnessed the souls of all four rise towards the heavens and the tragic tale of the sons of Tuirenn was recounted from

Opposite: His answer was severe and merciless: 'Let them die in the knowledge that they have achieved something good because of me.'

that day onwards throughout the land, becoming known as one of the Three Sorrows of Story-Telling.

The Tragedy of the Children of Lir

DURING THE GREAT BATTLE OF TAILTIU that raged on the plain of Moytura, the Tuatha De Danann were slain in vast numbers and finally defeated by a race of Gaelic invaders known as the Milesians. Following this time of wretched warring, Erin came to be divided into two separate kingdoms. The children of Miled claimed for themselves all the land above ground, while the Tuatha De Danann were banished to the dark regions below the earth's surface. The Danann gods did not suffer their defeat easily, and immediately set about re-building an impressive underground kingdom worthy of the divine stature they once possessed. Magnificent palaces, sparkling with jewels and precious stones, were soon erected and a world of wondrous beauty and light was created where once darkness had prevailed. Time had no meaning in this new domain and all who lived there remained eternally beautiful, never growing old as mortals did above ground.

The day approached for the Tuatha De Danann to choose for themselves a King who would safeguard their future peace and happiness. The principle deities and elders of the people gathered together at the Great Assembly and began deliberating on their choice of leader. Lir, father of the sea-god, Manannan mac Lir, had announced his desire to take the throne, but so too had Bodb the Red, son of the divinity Dagda, lord of perfect knowledge. It came to pass that the People of Dana chose Bodb the Red as their King and built for him a splendid castle on the banks of Loch Dearg. The new ruler made a solemn pledge to his people, promising to prove himself worthy of the great honour bestowed on him. Before long, the People of Dana began to applaud themselves on their choice. Their lives were happy and fulfilled and their kingdom flourished as never before.

Only one person in the entire land remained opposed to the new sovereign. Lir was highly offended that he had not been elected by the People of Dana. Retreating to his home at Sídh Fionnachaidh, he refused to acknowledge Bodb the Red, or show him any mark of respect. Several of the elders urged the King to gather his army together and march to Armagh where Lir could be punished for this insult, but Bodb the Red would not be persuaded. He desired more

Opposite: As each one of the children entered the water, Aoife struck them with her druidic wand, transforming them into milk-white swans.

than anything to be reconciled to every last one of his subjects and his warm and generous spirit sought a more compassionate way of drawing Lir back into his circle.

One morning, the King received news that Lir's wife had recently passed away, leaving him grief-stricken and despondent. Many had tried, but none had yet managed to improve Lir's troubled heart and mind and it was said that he would never recover from his loss. Bodb the Red immediately sent a message to Lir, inviting him to attend the palace. Deeply moved by the King's forgiveness and concern, Lir graciously accepted the invitation to visit Loch Dearg. A large banquet was prepared in his honour and four shining knights on horseback were sent forth to escort the chariot through the palace gates. The King greeted Lir warmly and sat him at the royal table at his right hand. The two men began to converse as if they had always been the closest of friends, and as the evening wore on it was noticed by all that the cloud of sorrow had lifted from Lir's brow. Presently, the King began to speak more earnestly to his friend of the need to return to happier times.

'I am sorely grieved to hear of your loss,' he told Lir, 'but you must allow me to help you. Within this court reside three of the fairest maidens in the kingdom. They are none other than my foster-daughters and

each is very dear to me. I give you leave to take the one you most admire as your bride, for I know that she will restore to your life the happiness you now lack.'

At the King's request, his three daughters entered the hall and stood before them. Their beauty was remarkable indeed, and each was as fair as the next. Lir's eyes travelled from one to the other in bewilderment. Finally, he settled on the daughter known as Aeb, for she was the eldest and deemed the wisest of the three. Bodb the Red gave the couple his blessing and it was agreed that they should be married without delay.

After seven days of glorious feasting and celebrating, Aeb and Lir set off from the royal palace to begin their new life together as husband and wife. Lir was no longer weighted down by sorrow and Aeb had grown to love and cherish the man who had chosen her as his bride. Many years of great joy followed for them both. Lir delighted in his new wife and in the twin children she bore him, a boy and a girl, whom they named Aed and Fionnguala. Within another year or two, Aeb again delivered of twins, two sons named Fiachra and Conn, but the second birth proved far more difficult and Aeb became gravely ill. Lir watched over her night and day. Yet despite his tender love and devotion, she could not be saved and his heart was again broken in two. The four beautiful children Aeb had borne him were his only solace in this great time of distress. During the worst moments, when he thought he would die of grief, he was rescued by their image and his love for them was immeasurable.

Hearing of Lir's dreadful misfortune, King Bodb offered him a second foster-daughter in marriage. Aeb's sister was named Aoife and she readily agreed to take charge of Lir's household and her sister's children. At first, Aoife loved her step-children as if they were her very own, but as she watched Lir's intense love for them increase daily, a feeling of jealousy began to take control of her. Often Lir would sleep in the same bed chamber with them and as soon as the children awoke, he devoted himself to their amusement, taking them on long hunting trips through the forest. At every opportunity, he kissed and embraced them and was more than delighted with the love he received in return. Believing that her husband no longer felt any affection for her, Aoife welcomed the poisonous and wicked thoughts that invaded her mind. Feigning a dreadful illness, she lay in bed for an entire year. She summoned a druid to her bedside and together they plotted a course to destroy Lir's children.

One day Aoife rose from her sickbed and ordered her chariot.

Opposite: Stunned and saddened by their step-mother's cruel act of vengeance, the Children of Lir bowed their heads and wept piteously for their fate.

Seeking out her husband in the palace gardens, she told him that she would like to take the children to visit her father, King Bodb. Lir was happy to see that his wife had recovered her health and was quick to encourage the outing. He gathered his children around him to kiss them goodbye, but Fionnguala refused her father's kiss and drew away from him, her eyes brimming with tears.

'Do not be troubled, child,' he spoke softly to her, 'your visit will bring the King great pleasure and he will prepare the most fleet-footed horses for your speedy return'.

Although her heart was in turmoil, Fionnguala mounted the chariot with her three brothers. She could not understand her sadness, and could not explain why it deepened with every turning of the chariot wheels as they moved forward, away from her father and her beloved home at Sídh Fionnachaidh.

When they had travelled some distance from Lir's palace, Aoife called the horses to a halt. Waking the children from their happy slumber, she ordered them out of the chariot and shouted harshly to her manservants:

'Kill these monstrous creatures before you, for they have stolen the love Lir once had for me. Do so quickly, and I shall reward you as you desire.'

But the servants recoiled in horror from her shameful request and replied resolutely:

'We cannot perform so terrible an evil. A curse will surely fall on you for even thinking such a vile thing.'

They journeyed on further until they approached the shores of Loch Dairbhreach. The evening was now almost upon them and a bank of deep crimson cloud hung lazily on the horizon above the shimmering lake. Weary starlings were settling in their nests and owls were preparing for their nocturnal watch. Aoife now sought to kill the children herself and drew from her cloak a long, pointed sabre. But as she raised her arm to slay the first of them, she was overcome by a feeling of maternal sympathy and it prevented her completing the task. Angry that she had been thwarted once more, she demanded that the children remove their garments and bathe in the lake. As each one them entered the water, she struck them with her druid's wand and they were instantly transformed into four milk-white swans. A death-like chill filled the air as she chanted over them the words the druid had taught her:

'Here on Dairbhreach's lonely wave
For years to come your watery home
Not Lir nor druid can now ye save
From endless wandering on the lonely foam.'

Stunned and saddened by their step-mother's cruel act of vengeance, the children of Lir bowed their heads and wept piteously for their fate. Fionnguala eventually found the courage to speak, and she uttered a plea for lenience, mindful of her three brothers and of the terrible tragedy Lir would again have to suffer:

'We have always loved you Aoife,' she urged, 'why have you treated us in this way when we have only ever shown you loyalty and kindness?'

So sad and helpless were Fionnguala's words, so soft and innocent was her childlike voice, that Aoife began to regret what she had done and she was suddenly filled with panic and despair. It was too late for her to undo her druid's spell, and it was all she could do to fix a term to the curse she had delivered upon the children:

'You will remain in the form of four white swans,' she told them, 'until a woman from the south shall be joined in marriage to a man from the north, and until the light of Christianity shines on Erin. For three hundred years you will be doomed to live on Loch Dairbhreach, followed by three hundred years on the raging Sea of Moyle, and a further three hundred years on Iorras Domhnann. I grant you the power of speech and the gift of singing, and no music in the world shall sound more beautiful and pleasing to the ear than that which you shall make.'

Then Aoife called for her horse to be harnessed once more and continued on her journey to the palace of Bodb the Red, abandoning the four white swans to their life of hardship on the grey and miserable moorland lake.

The King, who had been eagerly awaiting the arrival of his grandchildren, was deeply disappointed to discover that they had not accompanied his daughter.

'Lir will no longer entrust them to you,' Aoife told him, 'and I have not the will to disobey his wishes.'

Greatly disturbed by this news, the King sent a messenger to Lir's palace, demanding an explanation for his extraordinary behaviour. A strange sense of foreboding had already entered Lir's soul and, on receiving the King's message, he became tormented with worry for his children's safety. He immediately called for his horse to be saddled and galloped away into the night in the direction of Loch Dearg. Upon his arrival at Bodb's palace, he was met by one of Aoife's servants who could not keep from him the terrible tale of his wife's treachery. The King was now also informed and Aoife was ordered to appear before them both. The evil expression in his daughter's eye greatly enraged the King and his wand struck violently, changing Aoife into a demon, destined to wander the cold and windy air until the very end of time.

Before the sun had risen the next morning, an anguished party had set off from the palace in search of Lir's children. Through the fog and mist they rode at great speed until the murky waters of Loch Dairbhreach appeared before them in the distance. It was Lir who first caught a glimpse of the four majestic white swans, their slender necks arched forwards towards the pebbled shore, desperately seeking the warm and familiar face of their father. As the swans swam towards him, they began to speak with gentle voices and he instantly recognized his own children in the sad, snow-white creatures. How Lir's heart ached at this woeful sight, and how his eyes wished to disbelieve the sorrowful scene he was forced to witness. He began to sob loudly and it seemed that his grief would never again be silenced.

'Do not mourn us, father,' whispered Fiachra comfortingly, 'your love will give us strength in our plight and we shall all be together one day.'

A beautiful, soothing music now infused the air, miraculously lifting the spirits of all who heard it. After a time, Lir and his companions fell into a gentle, peaceful sleep and when they awoke they were no longer burdened by troubles. Every day, Lir came to visit his children and so too did the Men of Erin, journeying from every part to catch even a single note of the beautiful melody of the swans.

Three hundred years passed pleasantly in this way, until the time arrived for the Children of Lir to bid farewell to the People of Dana and to move on to the cold and stormy Sea of Moyle. As the stars faded and the first rays of sunlight peered through the heavens, Lir came forward to the shores of the lake and spoke to his children for the very last time. Fionnguala began to sing forlornly of the grim and bitter times which lay ahead and as she sang she spread her wings and rose from the water. Aed, Fiachra and Conn joined in her song and then took to the air as their sister had done, flying wearily over the velvet surface of Loch Dairbhreach towards the north-east and the raging ocean:

Arise, my brothers, from Dairbhreach's wave,
On the wings of the southern wind;
We leave our father and friends today
In measureless grief behind.
Ah! Sad the parting, and sad our flight.

To Moyle's tempestuous main;
For the day of woe
Shall come and go
Before we meet again!

Great was the suffering and hardship endured by the swans on the lonely Sea of Moyle, for they could find no rest or shelter from the hissing waves and the piercing cold of the wintry gales. During that first desolate winter, thick black clouds perpetually gathered in the sky, causing the sea to rise up in fury as they ruptured and spilled forth needles of icy rain and sleet. The swans were tossed and scattered by storms and often driven miles apart. There were countless nights when Fionnguala waited alone and terrified on the Rock of Seals, tortured with anxiety for the welfare of her brothers. The gods had so far answered her prayers and they had been returned to her on each occasion, drenched and battered. Tears of joy and relief flowed freely from her eyes at these times, and she would take her brothers under her wing and pull them to her breast for warmth.

Three hundred years of agony and misery on the Sea of Moyle were interrupted by only one happy event. It happened that one morning, the swans were approached by a group of horsemen while resting in the mouth of the river Bann. Two of the figures introduced themselves as Fergus and Aed, sons of Bodb the Red, and they were accompanied by a fairy host. They had been searching a good many years for the swans, desiring to bring them happy tidings of Lir and the King. The Tuatha De Danann were all now assembled at the annual Feast of Age, peaceful and happy, except for the deep sorrow they felt at the absence of the four children of Lir. Fionnguala and her brothers received great comfort from this visit and talked long into the evening with the visitors. When the time finally came for the men to depart, the swans felt that their courage had been restored and looked forward to being reunited with the People of Dana sometime in the future.

When at last their exile had come to an end on the Sea of Moyle, the children of Lir made ready for their voyage westwards to Iorras

Domhnann. In their hearts they knew they were travelling from one bleak and wretched place to another, but they were soothed by the thought that their suffering would one day be over. The sea showed them no kindness during their stay at Iorras Domhnann, and remained frozen from Achill to Erris during the first hundred years. The bodies of the swans became wasted from thirst and hunger, but they weathered the angry blasts of the tempests and sought shelter from the driving snow under the black, unfriendly rocks, refusing to give up hope. Each new trial fired the desire within them to be at home once again, safe in the arms of their loving father.

It was a time of great rejoicing among Lir's children when the three hundred years on Iorras Domhnann finally came to an end. With hearts full of joy and elation, the four swans rose ecstatically into the air and flew southwards towards Sídh Fionnachaidh, their father's palace. But their misery and torment was not yet at an end. As they circled above the plains of Armagh, they could not discover any trace of their former home. Swooping closer to the ground, they recognized the familiar grassy slopes of their childhood, but these were now dotted with stones and rubble from the crumbling castle walls. A chorus of wailing and sorrow echoed through the ruins of Lir's palace as the swans flung themselves on the earth, utterly broken and defeated. For three days and three nights they remained here until they could bear it no longer. Fionnguala led her brothers back to the west and they alighted on a small, tranquil lake known as Inis Gluare. All that remained was for them to live out the rest of their lives in solitude, declaring their grief through the saddest of songs.

On the day after the children of Lir arrived at Inis Gluare, a Christian missionary known as Chaemóc was walking by the lakeside where he had built for himself a small church. Hearing the haunting strains floating towards him from the lake, he paused by the water's edge and prayed that he might know who it was that made such stirring music. The swans then revealed themselves to him and began to tell him their sorry tale. Chaemóc bade them come ashore and he joined the swans together with silver chains and took them into his home where he tended them and provided for them until they had forgotten all their suffering. The swans were his delight and they joined him in his prayers and religious devotions, learning of the One True God who had come to save all men.

It was not long afterwards that Deoch, daughter of the King of Munster, came to marry Lairgnéan, King of Connacht, and hearing of Chaemóc's four wonderful swans, she announced her desire to have them as her wedding-present. Lairgnéan set off for Inis Gluare intent on seizing the swans from Chaemóc. Arriving at the church where they were resting, their heads bowed in silent prayer, he began to drag them from the altar. But he had not gone more than four paces when the plumage dropped from the birds and they were changed back into their human form. Three withered old men and a white-faced old woman now stood before Lairgnéan and he turned and fled in horror at the sight of them.

For the children of Lir had now been released from Aoife's curse, having lived through almost a thousand years, to the time when her prophecy came to be fulfilled. Knowing that they had little time left to them, they called for Chaemóc to baptize them and as he did so they died peacefully and happily. The saint carried their bodies to a large tomb and Fionnguala was buried at the centre, surrounded by her three beloved brothers. Chaemóc placed a large headstone on the mound and he inscribed it in oghram. It read, 'Lir's children, who rest here in peace at long last'.

The Wooing of Etain

MIDHIR THE PROUD was King of the Daoine Sidhe, the fairy people of the Tuatha De Danann, and he dwelt at the grand palace in the Hollow Hills of Brí Leíth. He had a wife named Fuamnach with whom he had lived quite contentedly for a good many years. One day, however, while Midhir was out hunting with a group of his companions, he stumbled across the fairest maiden he had ever before laid eyes on, resting by a mountain stream. She had begun to loosen her hair to wash it and her chestnut tresses fell about her feet, shimmering magnificently in the sunlight. The King was enraptured by her perfect beauty and grace and he could not prevent himself from instantly falling in love with her. Nothing could persuade him to abandon the thought of returning to the palace with the maiden and making her his new wife. He boldly confessed to her this desire, hopeful that his noble bearing and royal apparel would not fail to win her approval. The maiden told him that her name was Etain. She was both honoured and delighted that the fairy king had requested her hand in marriage and agreed at once to return with him to Brí Leíth.

Opposite:
Midhir the Proud was captivated by the maiden's beauty. She told him her name was Etain and agreed at once to return with him to Brí Leíth.

Within a short time, Etain's beauty had won her great fame throughout the land and the words 'as fair as Etain' became the highest compliment any man could bestow on a woman. Midhir had soon forgotten about his former wife and spent his days in the company of

his new bride whom he doted on and could not bear to be parted from. Fuamnach was distressed and enraged to see them together, but her desire to be comforted and loved once more was entirely overlooked by her husband. When she could bear her cruel treatment no longer, she sought the help of the druid, Bressal, who was well known to the royal palace. Bressal heard Fuamnach's story and took great pity on her. That evening, as Etain lay in bed, they both entered her chamber. A great tempest began to rage around them as the druid waved his wand over the sleeping woman and delivered his curse in grave, commanding tones. As soon as he had uttered his final words, the beautiful Etain was changed into a butterfly and swiftly carried off by the howling winds through the open window far beyond the palace of Midhir the Proud.

For seven long years, Etain lived a life of intolerable misery. She could find no relief from her endless flight and her delicate wings were tattered and torn by the fiery gusts that tossed and buffeted her throughout the length and breadth of the country. One day, when she had almost abandoned hope of ever finding rest again, a chance flurry thrust her through a window of the fairy palace of Aengus Óg, the Danann god of love. All deities of the Otherworld possessed the ability to recognize their own kind, and Etain was immediately revealed to Aengus, despite her winged appearance. He could not entirely undo the druid's sorcery, but he took Etain into his care and conjured up a spell to return her to her human form every day, from dusk until dawn. During the daytime, Aengus set aside the sunniest corner of the palace gardens for her private use and planted it with the most colourful, fragrant flowers and shrubs. In the evening, when Etain was transformed once again into a beautiful maiden, she gave Aengus her love and they grew to treasure each other's company, believing they would spend many happy years together.

It was not long, however, before Fuamnach came to discover Etain's place of refuge. Still bent on revenge, she appeared at the palace of Aengus Óg in the form of a raven and alighted on an apple tree in the centre of the garden. She soon caught sight of a dainty butterfly resting on some rose petals and with a sudden swoop she opened her beak

Opposite:
Throughout the winter months that followed, Etain remained haunted by the image of the stranger who had visited her on the hill.

and lifted the fragile creature into the air. Once they were outside of the palace walls, a magic tempest began to blow around Etain. She found herself being carried away from the fairy mounds during the fierce storm, to the unfamiliar plains of Erin above ground where very few of the fairy people had ever dared to emerge.

As soon as he discovered that Etain had been outwitted by
Fuamnach, Aengus sprinkled a magic potion into the air and called upon
the gods to end the beautiful maiden's torturous wanderings above the
earth's surface. A short time afterwards, Etain became trapped in a terrible
gale and was hurled through the castle windows of an Ulster Chieftain
named Etar. A great feast was in progress and all the noblemen of the
province were gathered together for an evening of merry-making and
dancing. Etar's wife sat at his right hand and she held a goblet of wine to her
lips. Weary and thirsty from her flight, Etain came to rest on the rim of the
vessel intending to sip some of the refreshing liquid. But as she leaned
forward, she fell into the drinking-cup and was passed down the throat of
the noblewoman as soon as she swallowed her next draught.

Several weeks after the great feast, Etar's wife was overjoyed to
discover that she was carrying a child. The gods had fulfilled their promise
and had caused Etain to nestle in her womb until the time when she could
be reborn as a mortal child. After nine months, the Chieftain and his wife

were blessed with a daughter and they gave her the name of Etain. She grew to become one of the most beautiful maidens in Ulster and although she bore the same name as before, she could remember nothing of her former life with the Daoine Sidhe.

It was at about this time that a distinguished warrior known as Eochaid Airem was crowned High King of Erin. One of the first tasks he set himself was to organize a splendid annual feast, gathering together all of the kingdom's noblemen to the royal palace for a month of glorious festivity. But the king was soon disappointed to discover that a great number of his noblemen would not accept his generous invitation. Deeply puzzled by this turn of events, he ordered several of them to appear before him and demanded an explanation.

'We cannot attend such a feast,' they told him, 'since the absence of a queen by your side would make it unwholesome. The people of Erin have never before served a king who does not possess a queen. There are many among us with daughters young and fair who would be more than willing to help restore your honour.'

The King was now made to realize that his integrity rested on securing a wife, and he immediately sent out horsemen to the four corners of Erin in search of a maiden who would make for him a suitable queen. Within a few days, a group of his messengers returned with the news that they had found the fairest creature in the land. Eochaid set forth at once to view with his own eyes the maiden his men had found for him. He rode for some distance until at last he happened upon four nymph-like figures laughing and dancing in the sunshine at the edge of a small, meandering brook. One of them was indeed far more beautiful than the others. She was clothed in a mantel of bright purple which was clasped over her bosom with a brooch of bright, glittering gold. Underneath, she wore a tunic of the finest emerald silk, intricately decorated with silver fringes and sparkling jewels. Her skin was as white and smooth as snow, her eyes were as blue as hyacinths and her lips as red as the finest rubies. Two tresses of chestnut hair rested on her head. Each one was plaited into four strands and fastened at the ends with tiny spheres of gold. Eochaid shyly approached the maiden and began to question her softly:

'Who are you,' he inquired, 'and who was it created so rare and beautiful a vision as you?'

'I am Etain, daughter of Etar,' said the maiden. 'Your messengers warned me of your visit Eochaid and I have heard noble tales of you since I was a little child.'

'Will you allow me to woo you then, fair Etain,' asked the King, 'for I cannot conceive of any greater pleasure left to me.'

'It is you I have waited for,' replied Etain, 'and I will only be truly fulfilled if you take me with you to Tara where I will serve you well as queen.'

Overwhelmed with joy at these words, Eochaid grasped Etain's hand and lifted her onto the saddle next to him. They rode speedily towards the palace at Tara where news of the king's betrothal had already reached the ears of his subjects. A hearty welcome awaited the couple as they approached the great gates and they were married that same afternoon to the jubilant sounds of chiming bells and shouts of approval from the large crowd that had gathered to wish them well.

The Royal Assembly of Tara was now the grand occasion everybody looked forward to and preparations began in earnest for the series of lavish banquets and pageants that were to take place in the grounds of the palace. On the morning of first day of the Assembly, Etain made ready to welcome Eochaid's guests and she rode to the top of the hill beyond the gates to catch a glimpse of the first to arrive. After a time, a young warrior on horseback appeared in the distance making his way steadily towards her. He wore a robe of royal purple and his hair, which tumbled below his shoulders, was golden yellow in colour. His face was proud and radiant and his eyes lustrous and gentle. In his left hand, he held a five-pointed spear and in his right, a circular shield, laden with white gold and precious gems. The warrior came forward and Etain welcomed him zealously:

'We are honoured by your presence, young warrior,' said Etain. 'A warm reception awaits you at the palace where I shall be pleased to lead you.'

But the warrior hesitated to accompany her and began to speak in a pained, anxious voice.

'Do you not know me, Etain?' he asked. 'For years I have been searching every corner of the land for you. I am your husband, Midhir the Proud, from the fairy kingdom of the Ever Young.'

'My husband is Eochaid Airem, High King of Erin,' replied Etain. 'Are you not deceived by your own eyes? You are a stranger to me and I have never before heard of your kingdom.'

'Fuamnach is dead and it is now safe for you to return to your home,' Midhir told her. 'It was the sorcery of Fuamnach and Bressal that drove us apart, Etain. Will you come with me now to a land full of music, where men and women remain eternally fair and without blemish. There, in the land of your birth, we may again live happily as man and wife.'

'I will not readily abandon the King of Erin for a man unknown to me,' answered Etain. 'I would never seek to depart with you without the King's consent and I know he will not give it, since his love for me deepens with every passing day.'

Hearing these words, Midhir bowed his head in defeat. It was not in his nature to take Etain by force and he sadly bade her farewell, galloping furiously across the plains of Erin, his purple cloak billowing around him in the breeze.

Throughout the winter months that followed, Etain remained haunted by the image of the stranger who had visited her on the hill. She began to dream of a land filled with sunshine and laughter where she frequently appeared seated on a throne, smiling happily. She could not explain these dreams and did not dare to confide in her husband. Often, however, she would ride to the place where she had met with Midhir the Proud and gaze outwards towards the flat, green carpet of land, secretly entertaining the hope that a rider on a white horse might suddenly appear on the horizon.

One fair summer's morning as Eochaid Airem peered out of the palace window, he noticed a young warrior in a purple cloak riding towards the Hill of Tara. The King was intrigued by the sight and ordered his horse to be saddled so that he might personally greet the stranger and establish the purpose of his visit to the palace.

'I am known to all as Midhir,' said the warrior. 'I have journeyed here to meet with Eochaid Airem, for I am told he is the finest chess-player in the land. I have with me a chessboard with which to test his skill if he is willing to meet my challenge.'

The warrior then produced from beneath his mantel a solid gold chessboard with thirty-two silver pieces, each one encrusted with the finest sapphires and diamonds.

'I would be more than delighted to play a game of chess with you,' replied the King, and he led the way to a brightly-lit chamber where they placed the board on a sturdy round table and sat down to play the first game. The King was not long in proving his reputation as a champion player and, as the young warrior seemed disappointed with his own performance, it was decided that they should play a second game. Again, the King was victorious and the warrior appeared to

Opposite: The young warrior's face was proud and radiant, his eyes lustrous and gentle. His hair, which tumbled below his shoulders, was golden yellow in colour.

become more and more agitated. But it was Midhir's intention all along to win Eochaid's sympathy and to lure him into a false sense of security.

'Perhaps it would be best,' suggested the King, 'if we decided on a wager for our third and final game. Name your stake, choose any treasure you desire, and it will be forfeited to you if you are triumphant over me.'

'That is very generous of you,' replied Midhir, 'but I have more than enough wealth and possessions to satisfy me. Perhaps you have a wife, however, who would not protest too loudly if I stole from her a single kiss as my prize?'

'I am sure she would not object,' answered Eochaid cheerfully, for he felt certain that Etain would never have to deliver such a trophy.

The two played on, but this time the King struggled to keep control of the game and at length he was beaten by the younger man. Eochaid now fell silent and began to regret that he had so carelessly offered his wife as prize. In desperation and despair, he begged his opponent to surrender his claim to the pledged kiss. But Midhir insisted firmly on the forfeit and the King was forced to honour his part of the bargain.

'Perhaps you will find it in your heart to show me a little kindness,' Eochaid pleaded, 'and allow me time to reconcile myself to the dispatch of such a precious reward. Return to this palace one month from today and what you have asked for will not be denied you.'

'Your request is not unreasonable,' replied Midhir, 'and it leads me to believe that a kiss from your wife must be worth the long wait.'

Then Eochaid Airem appointed a day at the end of the month when Midhir would return to collect his prize and the young warrior departed the palace, his heart lighter than it had been for a very long time.

As the days passed by and the time approached for Etain to deliver her kiss, the King became more and more protective of his beautiful wife. Fearing that his handsome rival would appear at any moment, he gave the order for the palace to be surrounded by a great host of armed men and instructed them not to allow any stranger to enter the grounds. Once he had made certain that the outer courtyards were protected and that the doors to the inner chambers were properly guarded, Eochaid began to feel more at ease and decided to invite his closest friends to dine with him later that evening in the banqueting hall. Etain appeared next to him in a gown of shimmering silver and a row of servants carried trays of the most exotic food and flagons of the finest wine through to the long table. While the queen poured the wine for her hosts, the hall began to fill with laughter and conversation and it was not long before Eochaid called for his musicians to begin playing.

In the midst of this happy atmosphere, nobody noticed the tall, elegant figure enter the room and make his way towards the King, his face noble and determined, his spear held proudly in his left hand. Etain suddenly raised her eyes and saw before her the young rider whose image had filled her sleeping hours since their meeting on the Hill of Tara. He appeared more beautiful and resplendent than ever, more eloquent and powerful than her memory had allowed for. A wonderful feeling of warmth and affection stirred within Etain's breast as Midhir gazed tenderly upon her and she felt that somehow she had always known and loved the man who stood before her. Then Midhir addressed the King and his words were purposeful and resolute:

'Let me collect what has been promised me,' he said to Eochaid, 'It is a debt that is due and the time is ripe for payment.'

The King and his party looked on helplessly as Midhir encircled the fair Etain in his arms. As their lips met, a thick veil of mist appeared around them, and they were lifted gracefully into the air and out into the night. Eochaid and his noblemen rushed from the banqueting hall in pursuit of the couple, but all they could see were two white swans circling the star-filled sky above the royal palace. Eochaid wept bitterly for his loss and swore solemnly that he would not rest a single moment until every fairy mound in the land had been dug up and destroyed in his search for Midhir the Proud.

* * *

THE ULSTER CYCLE
STORIES OF CUCHULAINN
OF THE RED GUARD

he Ulster Cycle, also known as the Red Branch Cycle, is compiled of tales of Ulster's traditional heroes, chief among whom is Cuchulainn[1], arguably the most important war-champion in ancient Irish literature. An account of his birth dating from the ninth century is retold here, although a great many variations exist.

From the age of six, Cuchulainn displays his supernatural ancestry and astounding strength. While still a child, he slays the terrifying hound of Culann. As a mere youth he is sent to train with the Knights of the Red Guard under Scathach and he alone is entrusted with the diabolical weapon known as the Gae Bolg. Later, he single-handedly defends Ulster against Queen Medb[2] while the rest of the province sleeps under the charm of Macha. His most notable exploits spanning his hectic warrior's life up until his early death are recounted here.

Cuchulainn is said to have fallen at the battle of Muirthemne, circa 12 BC. He was finally overcome by his old enemy Lugaid, aided by the monstrous daughters of Calatin. As death approaches, Cuchulainn insists that he be allowed to bind himself upright to a pillar-stone. With his dying breath, he gives a loud, victorious laugh and when Lugaid attempts to behead his corpse, the enemy's right hand is severed as the sword of Cuchulainn falls heavily upon it. The hero's death is avenged by Conall the Victorious, but with the defeat of Cuchulainn, the end is sealed to the valiant reign of the Red Guard Knights in ancient Irish legend.

[1] Pronounced Koo khul-in.
[2] Pronounced Maev.

The Birth of Cuchulainn

KING CONCHOBAR MAC NESSA was ruler of Ulster at the time when Cuchulainn, the mightiest hero of the Red Guard, came to be born. It happened that one day, the King's sister Dechtire, whom he cherished above all others, disappeared from the palace without warning, taking fifty of her maidens and her most valuable possessions with her. Although Conchobar summoned every known person in the court before him for questioning, no explanation could be discovered for his sister's departure. For three long years, the King's messengers scoured the country in search of Dechtire, but not one among them ever brought him news of her whereabouts.

At last, one summer's morning, a strange flock of birds descended on the palace gardens of Emain Macha and began to gorge themselves on every fruit tree and vegetable patch in sight. Greatly disturbed by the greed and destruction he witnessed, the King immediately gathered together a party of his hunters, and they set off in pursuit of the birds, armed with powerful slings and the sharpest of arrows. Fergus mac Roig, Conchobar's chief huntsman and guide, was among the group, as were his trusted warriors Amergin and Bricriu. As the day wore on, they found themselves being lured a great distance southward by the birds, across Sliab Fuait, towards the Plain of Gossa, and with every step taken they grew more angry and frustrated that not one arrow had yet managed to ruffle a single feather.

Nightfall had overtaken them before they had even noticed the light begin to fade, and the King, realizing that they would never make it safely back to the palace, gave the order for Fergus and some of the others to go out in search of a place of lodging for the party. Before long, Fergus came upon a small hut whose firelight was extremely inviting, and he approached and knocked politely on the door. He received a warm and hearty welcome from the old married couple within, and they at once offered him food and a comfortable bed for the evening. But Fergus would not accept their kind hospitality, knowing that his companions were still abroad without shelter.

Opposite: The King, realizing that they would never make it safely back, ordered Fergus and some of the others to go out in search of a place of lodging for the party.

'Then they are all invited to join us,' said the old woman, and as she bustled about, preparing food and wine for her visitors, Fergus went off to deliver his good news to Conchobar and the rest of the group.

Bricriu had also set off in search of accommodation, and as he had walked to the opposite side of the woodlands, he was certain

 CELTIC MYTHS & LEGENDS

that he heard the gentle sound of harp music. Instinctively drawn towards the sweet melody, he followed the winding path through the trees until he came upon a regal mansion standing proudly on the banks of the river Boyne. He timidly approached the noble structure, but there was no need for him to knock, since the door was already ajar and a young maiden, dressed in a flowing gown of shimmering gold, stood in the entrance hall ready to greet him. She was accompanied by a young man of great stature and splendid appearance who smiled warmly at Bricriu and extended his hand in friendship:

'You are indeed welcome,' said the handsome warrior, 'we have been waiting patiently for your visit to our home this day.'

'Come inside, Bricriu,' said the beautiful maiden, 'why is it that you linger out of doors?'

'Can it be that you do not recognize the woman who appears before you?' asked the warrior.

'Her great beauty stirs a memory from the past,' replied Bricriu, 'but I cannot recall anything more at present.'

'You see before you Dechtire, sister of Conchobar mac Nessa,' said the warrior, 'and the fifty maidens you have been seeking these three years are also in this house. They have today visited Emain Macha in the form of birds in order to lure you here.'

'Then I must go at once to the King and inform him of what I have discovered,' answered Bricriu, 'for he will be overjoyed to know that Dechtire has been found and will be eager for her to accompany him back to the palace where there will be great feasting and celebration.'

He hurried back through the woods to rejoin the King and his companions. And when Conchobar heard the news of Bricriu's discovery, he could scarcely contain his delight and was immediately anxious to be reunited with his sister. A messenger was sent forth to invite Dechtire and the warrior to share in their evening meal, and a place was hurriedly prepared for the couple at the table inside the welcoming little hut. But Dechtire was already suffering the first pangs of childbirth by the time Conchobar's messenger arrived with his invitation. She excused herself by saying that she was tired and agreed instead to meet up with her brother at dawn on the following morning.

When the first rays of sunshine had brightened the heavens, Conchobar arose from his bed and began to prepare himself for Dechtire's arrival. He had passed a very peaceful night and went in

Opposite: The King's sister Dechtire, whom he cherished above all others, had disappeared from the palace without warning, taking fifty of her maidens with her.

 60

search of Fergus and the others in the happiest of moods. Approaching the place where his men were sleeping, he became convinced that he had heard the stifled cries of an infant. Again, as he drew nearer, the sound was repeated. He stooped down and began to examine a small, strange bundle lying on the ground next to Bricriu. As he unwrapped it, the bundle began to wriggle in his arms and a tiny pink hand revealed itself from beneath the cloth covering.

Dechtire did not appear before her brother that morning, or on any morning to follow. But she had left the King a great gift – a newborn male child fathered by the noble warrior, Lugh of the Long Arm, a child destined to achieve great things for Ulster. Conchobar took the infant back to the palace with him and gave him to his sister Finnchoem to look after. Finnchoem reared the child alongside her own son Conall and grew to love him as if he had been born of her own womb. He was given the name of Setanta, a name he kept until the age of six, and the druid Morann made the following prophecy over him:

His praise will be sung by the most valorous knights,
And he will win the love of all
His deeds will be known throughout the land
For he will answer Ulster's call.

How Setanta Won the Name of Cuchulainn

WITHIN THE COURT OF EMAIN MACHA, there existed an élite group of boy athletes whose outstanding talents filled the King with an overwhelming sense of pride and joy. It had become a regular part of Conchobar's daily routine to watch these boys at their various games and exercises, for nothing brought him greater pleasure than to witness their development into some of the finest sportsmen in Erin. He had named the group the Boy-Corps, and the sons of the most powerful chieftains and princes of the land were among its members, having proven their skill and dexterity in a wide and highly challenging range of sporting events.

Opposite: There was not a hound in Erin that could equal Culann's for fierceness and strength. Not even a hundred men could hope to overcome it.

Before Setanta had grown to the age of six, he had already expressed his desire before the King to be enrolled in the Boy-Corps. At first, Conchobar refused to treat the request seriously, since his nephew was a great deal younger than any other member, but the boy persisted, and the King at last agreed to allow him to try his hand. It was decided that he should join in a game of hurling one morning, and when he had dressed himself in the martial uniform of the Boy-Corps, he was presented with a brass hurley almost his own height off the ground.

A team of twelve boys was assembled to play against him and they sneered mockingly at the young lad before them, imagining they would have little difficulty keeping the ball out of his reach. But as soon as the game started up, Setanta dived in among the boys and took hold of the ball, striking it with his hurley and driving it a powerful distance to the other end of the field where it sailed effortlessly through the goal-posts. And after this first onslaught, he made it impossible for his opponents to retrieve the ball from him, so that within a matter of minutes he had scored fifty goals against the twelve of them. The whole corps looked on in utter amazement and the King, who had been eagerly following the game, was flushed with excitement. His nephew's show of prowess was truly astonishing and he began to reproach himself for having originally set out to humour the boy.

'Have Setanta brought before me,' he said to his steward, 'for such an impressive display of heroic strength and impertinent courage deserves a very special reward.'

Now on that particular day, Conchobar had been invited to attend a great feast at the house of Culann, the most esteemed craftsman and smith in the kingdom. A thought had suddenly entered Conchobar's head that it would be a very fitting reward for Setanta to share in such a banquet, for no small boy had ever before accompanied the King and the Knights of the Red Guard on such a prestigious outing. It was indeed a great honour and

one Setanta readily acknowledged. He desperately wanted to accept the invitation, but only one thing held him back. He could not suppress the desire of a true sportsman to conclude the game he had begun and pleaded with the King to allow him to do so:

'I have so thoroughly enjoyed the first half of my game with the Boy-Corps,' he told the King, 'that I am loathe to cut it short. I promise to follow when the game is over if you will allow me this great liberty.'

And seeing the excitement and keenness shining in the boy's eyes, Conchobar was more than happy to agree to this request. He instructed Setanta to follow on before nightfall and gave him directions to the house of Culann. Then he set off for the banquet, eager to relate the morning's stirring events to the rest of Culann's house guests.

It was early evening by the time the royal party arrived at the dwelling place of Culann. A hundred blazing torches guided them towards the walls of the fort and a carpet of fresh green rushes formed a mile-long path leading to the stately entrance. The great hall was already lavishly prepared for the banquet and the sumptuous aroma of fifty suckling pigs turning on the spit filled every room of the house. Culann himself came forward to greet each one of his guests and he bowed respectfully before the King and led him to his place of honour at the centre of the largest table. Once his royal guest had taken his seat, the order was given for the wine to be poured and the laughter and music followed soon afterwards. And when it was almost time for the food to be served, Culann glanced around him one last time to make certain that all his visitors had arrived.

'I think we need wait no longer,' he said to the King. 'My guests are all present and it will now be safe to untie the hound who keeps watch over my home each night. There is not a hound in Erin who could equal mine for fierceness and strength, and even if a hundred men should attempt to do battle with him, every last one would be torn to pieces in his powerful jaws.'

'Release him then, and let him guard this place,' said Conchobar, quite forgetting that his young nephew had not yet joined the party. 'My men are all present and our appetites have been whetted by our long journey here. Let us delay no longer and begin the feasting at once.'

And after the gong had been sounded, a procession of elegantly-clad

attendants entered the room carrying gilded trays of roasted viands and freshly harvested fruit and vegetables, which they set down on the table before the King and the hungry warriors of the Red Guard.

It was just at this moment that the young Setanta came to the

green of Culann's fort carrying with him the hurley and the ball that had brought him victory against the Boy-Corps. As the boy drew nearer to the entrance of the fort, the hound's ears pricked up warily and it began to growl and bark in such a way as to be heard throughout the entire country-side. The whole company within the great hall heard the animal snarling ferociously and raced outdoors to discover what exactly it was that had disturbed the creature. They saw before them a young boy, who showed little sign of fear as he stood facing the fierce dog with gaping jaws. The child was without any obvious weapon of defence against the animal, but as it charged at him, he thrust his playing ball forcefully down its throat causing it to choke for breath. Then he seized the hound by the hind legs and dashed its head against a rock until blood spewed from its mouth and the life had gone out of it.

Those who witnessed this extraordinary confrontation hoisted the lad triumphantly into the air and bore him on their shoulders to where Conchobar and Culann stood waiting. The King, although more than gratified by the boy's demonstration of courage, was also much relieved to know that Setanta was safe. Turning to his host, he began to express his joy, but it was immediately apparent that Culann could share none of Conchobar's happiness. He walked instead towards the body of his dead hound and fell into a mournful silence as he stroked the lifeless form, remembering the loyal and obedient animal who had given its life to protect its master's property. Seeing Culann bent over the body of his faithful dog, Setanta came forward without hesitation and spoke the following words of comfort to him:

'If in all of Erin there is a hound to replace the one you have lost, I will find it, nurture it and place it in your service when it is fit for action. But, in the meantime, I myself will perform the duty of that hound and will guard your land and your possessions with the utmost pride.'

There was not one among the gathering who remained unmoved by this gesture of contrition and friendship. Culann, for his part, was overcome with gratitude and appreciation and declared that Setanta should bear the name of Cuchulainn, 'Culann's Hound', in remembrance of his first great act of valour. And so, at the age of six, the boy Setanta was named Cuchulainn, a name by which he was known and feared until the end of his days.

The Tragedy of Cuchulainn and Connla

AS SOON AS CUCHULAINN had reached the appropriate age to begin his formal training as a Knight of the Red Guard, it was decided at the court of Conchobar mac Nessa that he should depart for the Land of Shadows, where Scathach, the wisest, strongest, most celebrated woman-warrior, had prepared the path of his instruction in the feats of war. The stronghold of Scathach lay in a mysterious land overseas, beyond the bounds of the Plain of Ill-luck. It could only be reached by crossing the Perilous Glen, a journey very few had survived, for the Glen teemed with the fiercest of goblins lying in wait to devour hopeful young pilgrims. But even if a youth managed to come through the Perilous Glen unharmed, he had then to cross the Bridge of Leaps, underneath which the sea boiled and hissed furiously. This bridge was the highest and narrowest ever built and it spanned the steepest gorge in the western world. Only a handful of people had ever crossed it, but those who did were privileged to become the highest ranking scholars of Scathach and the very finest of Erin's warriors.

Within a week of leaving the court of Emain Macha, Cuchulainn had arrived at the Plain of Ill-luck and although he had already suffered many trials along the way, he knew in his heart that the worst still lay ahead. As he gazed out over the vast stretch of barren land he was obliged to traverse, he grew despondent, for he could see that one half was covered in a porous clay which would certainly cause his feet to stick fast, while the other was overgrown with long, coarse, straw-coloured grass, whose pointed blades were designed to slash a man's limbs to pieces. And as he stood crestfallen, attempting to decide which of the two routes would prove less hazardous, he noticed a young man approaching on horseback from the east. The very appearance of the rider lifted Cuchulainn's spirits, but when he observed that the youth's countenance shone as splendidly as the golden orb of the sun (though he does not reveal himself, this is, of course, Cuchulainn's father, Lugh of the Long Arm), he immediately felt hopeful and reassured once more. The two began to converse together and Cuchulainn enquired of the young man which track he considered the best to follow across the Plain of Ill-luck. The youth pondered the question awhile and then, reaching beneath his mantel, he handed Cuchulainn a leather pouch containing a small golden wheel.

'Roll this before you as you cross the quagmire,' he told

Cuchulainn, 'and it will scorch a path in the earth which you may follow safely to the stronghold of Scathach.'

Cuchulainn gratefully received the gift and bid farewell to the youth. And after he had set the wheel in motion, it led him safely, just as the young rider had promised, across the Plain of Ill-luck and through the Perilous Glen until he reached the outskirts of the Land of Shadows.

It was not long before he happened upon a small camp in the heart of the woodlands where the scholars of Scathach, the sons of the noblest princes and warriors of Erin, were busy at their training. He recognized at once his friend Ferdia, son of the Firbolg, Daman, and the two men embraced each other warmly. After Cuchulainn had told Ferdia all of the latest news from Ulster, he began to question his friend about the great woman-warrior who was set to educate him in arms.

'She dwells on the island beyond the Bridge of Leaps,' Ferdia told him, 'which no man, not even myself, has ever managed to cross. It is said that when we have achieved a certain level of valour, Scathach herself will teach us to cross the bridge, and she will also teach us to thrust the Gae Bolg, a weapon reserved for only the bravest of champions.'

'Then I must prove to her that I am already valorous,' replied Cuchulainn, 'by crossing that bridge without any assistance from her.'

'You are unlikely to succeed,' warned Ferdia, 'for if a man steps on one end of the bridge, the middle rises up and flings him into the waters below where the mouths of sea-monsters lie open, ready to swallow him whole.'

But these words of caution merely fired Cuchulainn's ambition to succeed in his quest. Retiring to a quiet place, he sat down to recover his strength from his long journey and waited anxiously for evening to fall.

The scholars of Scathach had all gathered to watch Cuchulainn attempt to cross the Bridge of Leaps and they began to jeer him loudly when after the third attempt he had failed to reach the far side. The mocking chorus that greeted his failure greatly infuriated the young warrior but prompted him at the same time to put all his strength and ability into one final, desperate leap. And at the fourth leap, which came to be known as 'the hero's salmon-leap', Cuchulainn landed on the ground of the island at the far side of the bridge. Lifting himself off the ground, he strode triumphantly to the fortress of Scathach and beat loudly on the entrance door with the shaft of his spear. Scathach appeared before him, wonder-struck that a boy so young and fresh of face had demon-

Opposite:
The stronghold of Scathach lay beyond the Perilous Glen, a glen teeming with the fiercest goblins lying in wait to devour hopeful young pilgrims.

strated such courage and vigour. She agreed at once to accept him as her pupil, promising to teach him all the feats of war if he would pledge himself to remain under her tuition and guidance for a period not less than a full year and a day.

During the time that Cuchulainn dwelt with Scathach, he grew to become her favourite pupil, for he acquired each new skill with the greatest of ease and approached every additional challenge set him with the utmost enthusiasm. Scathach had never before deemed any of her students good enough to be trained in the use of the Gae Bolg, but she now considered Cuchulainn a champion worthy of this special honour and presented him one morning with the terrible weapon. Then she instructed him on how to use it and explained that it should be hurled with the foot, and upon entering the enemy it would fill every inch of his body with deadly barbs, killing him almost instantly.

It was while Cuchulainn remained under Scathach's supervision that the Land of Shadows came under attack from the fiercest of tribal warriors, led by the Princess Aife. After several weeks of bloody battle, during which no solution to the conflict could be reached, it was agreed that Scathach and Aife should face each other in single combat. On hearing this news, Cuchulainn expressed the gravest concern and was adamant that he would accompany Scathach to the place where the contest was due to take place. Yet Scathach feared that something untoward might befall her young protégé, and she placed a sleeping-potion in Cuchulainn's drink with the power to prevent him waking until she was safely reached her meeting place with Aife. But the potion, which would have lasted twenty-four hours in any other man, held Cuchulainn in a slumber for less than one hour and when he awoke he seized his weapon and went forth to join the war against Aife.

And not only did he slay three of Aife's finest warriors in the blink of an eyelid, he insisted on trading places with Scathach and facing the tribal-leader by himself. But before going into battle against her, he asked Scathach what it was that Aife prized above all other things.

'What she most loves are her two horses, her chariot, and her charioteer,' she informed Cuchulainn. So he set off to meet Aife, forearmed with this knowledge.

Opposite: Scathach placed a sleeping-potion in Cuchulainn's drink, but the potion held him in a slumber for less than one hour.

The two opponents met on the Path of Feats and entered into a vicious combat there. They had only clashed swords three or four times however, before Aife delivered Cuchulainn a mighty blow, shattering his powerful sword to the hilt and leaving him defenceless.

Seeing the damage to his weapon, Cuchulainn at once cried out:

'What a terrible fate that charioteer beyond has met with. Look, his chariot and his two beautiful horses have fallen down the glen.'

And as Aife glanced around, Cuchulainn managed to seize her by the waist, squeezing firmly with his hands until she could hardly breathe and had dropped her sword at his feet. Then he carried her over his shoulder back to the camp of Scathach and flung her on the ground where he placed his knife at her throat.

'Do not take my life from me, Cuchulainn,' Aife begged, 'and I will agree to whatever you demand.'

It was soon settled between Scathach and Cuchulainn that Aife should agree to a lasting peace and, as proof of her commitment, they pronounced that she should bind herself over to remain a full year as Cuchulainn's hostage in the Land of Shadows. And after nine months, Aife gave birth to a son whom she named Connla, for she and Cuchulainn had grown to become the best of friends and the closest of lovers with the passing of time.

Now sadly, the day arrived for Cuchulainn to depart the Land of Shadows, and knowing that Aife would not accompany him, he spoke the following wish for his son's future:

'I give you this golden ring for our child,' he told Aife. 'And when he has grown so that the ring fits his finger, send him away from here to seek out his father in Erin.

'Counsel him on my behalf to keep his identity secret,' he added, 'so that he may stand proud on his own merit and never refuse a combat, or turn out of his way for any man.'

Then after he had uttered these words, Cuchulainn took his leave of Aife and made his way back to his own land and his people.

Seven years had passed, during which time Cuchulainn had chosen Emer, daughter of Forgall, one of the finest maidens in Ulster, to become his wife, and the two lived a very happy life together. He rarely thought of Aife and the son he had left behind in the Land of Shadows, for he had also risen to become captain of the House of the Red Branch of Conchobar mac Nessa and was by far the busiest and most respected warrior in the kingdom.

It was at this time, however, that Connla, son of Cuchulainn, set out on his journey to be reunited with his father in Erin, approaching her shores on the precise day that all the great warriors and noble

Opposite: Scathach, the most cunning and terrible of warrior women had taught the mighty Cuchulainn in the feats of war.

lords of Ulster were assembled for an annual ceremony on the Strand of Footprints. They were very much surprised to see a little boat of bronze appear on the crest of the waves, and in it a small boy clutching a pair of gilded oars, steering his way steadily towards them. The boy seemed not to notice them and every so often he stopped rowing and bent down to pick up a stone from the heap he had collected at the bottom of the boat. Then, putting one of these stones into a sling, he launched a splendid shot at the sea-birds above, bringing the creatures down, stunned, but unharmed, one after another, in a manner far too quick for the naked eye to perceive. The whole party looked on in amazement as the lad performed these wonderful feats, but the King soon grew uncomfortable at the spectacle he witnessed and called Condere, son of Eochaid, to him:

'This boy's arrival here does not bode well for us,' said the King. 'For if grown-up men of his kind were to follow in his wake, they would grind us all to dust. Let someone go to meet him and inform him that he is not welcome on Erin's soil.'

And as the boy came to moor his boat, Condere approached him and delivered Conchobar's message.

'Go and tell your King,' said the boy, 'that even if everyone among you here had the strength of a hundred men, and you all came forward to challenge me, you would not be able to persuade me to turn back from this place.'

Hearing these words, the King grew even more concerned and he called Conall the Victorious to him:

'This lad mocks us,' Conchobar told him, 'and it is now time for a show of force against him.'

So Conall was sent against the boy, but as he approached the lad put a stone in his sling and sent it whizzing with a noise like thunder through the air. It struck Conall on the forehead, knocking him backwards to the ground and before he could even think about rising to his feet, the boy had bound his arms and legs with the strap from his shield. And in this manner, the youth made a mockery of the host of Ulster, challenging man after man to confront him, and succeeding on every occasion to defeat his opponents

Opposite:
Aife gave birth to a son whom she named Connla, for she and Cuchulainn had grown to become the best of friends and the closest of lovers.

with little or no effort.

At last, when King Conchobar could suffer this humiliation no longer, he sent a messenger to Dundalk to the house of Cuchulainn requesting that he come and do battle against the young boy whom Conall the Victorious could not even manage to overcome. And hearing

that her husband was prepared to meet this challenge, Emer, his wife, went and pleaded with him not to go forward to the Strand of Footprints:

'Do not go against the boy,' she begged Cuchulainn, 'since the great courage he possesses has convinced me that he is Connla, son of Aife. Hear my voice, Cuchulainn, and do not go forward to murder your only child.'

'Even if he were my son,' replied Cuchulainn, 'I would slay him for the honour of Ulster.'

And he ordered his chariot to be yoked without further delay and set off in the direction of the strand.

Soon afterwards, he came upon the young boy sitting in his boat polishing stones and calmly awaiting his next opponent. Cuchulainn strode towards him, demanding to know his name and lineage. But the boy would not reveal his identity or the slightest detail of the land of his birth. Then Cuchulainn lost patience with him and they began to exchange blows. With one daring stroke, the boy cut off a lock of Cuchulainn's hair, and as he watched it fall to the ground, the older warrior became greatly enraged.

'Enough of this child's play,' he shouted and, dragging the boy from the boat, he began to wrestle with him in the water. But the boy's strength was astonishing and he managed twice to push Cuchulainn's head beneath the waves, almost causing him to drown. And it was on the third occasion that this occurred, when Cuchulainn gasped helplessly for air, that he remembered the Gae Bolg which Scathach had entrusted him with, and he flung it at the boy through the water. At once, the boy loosened his powerful hold and reached agonizingly towards his stomach, where the blood flowed freely from the vast gaping wound the weapon had made there.

'That is a weapon Scathach has not yet taught me to use,' said the boy. 'Carry me now from the water, for I am gravely injured.'

And as Cuchulainn bore the boy in his arms towards the shore he noticed a golden ring on his middle finger.

'It is true then,' he murmured sadly to himself, and set the boy down on the ground before the King and the men of Ulster.

'You see here before you my son,' Cuchulainn announced solemnly, 'the child I have mortally wounded for the good of Ulster.'

Opposite: Cuchulainn had chosen Emer, daughter of Forgall, one of the finest maidens in Ulster, to become his wife.

'Alas, it is so,' spoke Connla in a feeble voice, 'and I wish with all my heart that I could remain with you to the end of five years. For in that time, I would grow among you and conquer the world before you on every side, so that soon you would rule as far as Rome. But

since this cannot be, let me now take my leave of the most famous among you before I die.'

So, one after another, the most courageous knights of the Red Guard were brought before Connla and he placed his arms around the neck of each of them and embraced them affectionately. Then Cuchulainn came forward and his son kissed his father tenderly before drawing his last breath. And as he closed his eyes, a great lament was raised among them and they dug a grave for the boy and set a splendid pillar-stone at its head. Connla, son of Aife, was the only son Cuchulainn ever had and he lived to regret for the rest of his days that he had destroyed so precious a gift.

The Combat of Ferdia and Cuchulainn

BEYOND THE BORDERS OF ULSTER in the province of Connacht, there ruled a spirited and domineering queen named Medb, daughter of Eochaid Fedlech, whose husband, King Ailill, was the meekest and gentlest of creatures. Medb's nature was such that whatever she desired she took for her own, and whatever law displeased her, she refused to obey, so that her husband gave her whatever she demanded and nothing was ever too great a task for him to complete on her behalf. Medb was also the strongest and mightiest of warriors and she had gathered together a powerful army, convinced that one day she would conquer the whole land of Erin.

One evening as Medb and her husband lay together, they began to count up and compare their numerous possessions, for it was one of Medb's favourite entertainments to ridicule Ailill by proving that she had acquired far more treasures and wealth than he had over the years. Weapons, rings and jewellery were counted out, as well as chariots, horses, mansions and plots of land, but each of them was found to possess precisely the same amount as the other. So they began to count the herds of cattle and sheep that roamed the pastures beyond the walls of the castle and it was then that Ailill remembered the Bull of Finnbennach and began to tease his wife

Opposite: It was one of Queen Medb's favourite entertainments to ridicule King Ailill by proving that she had acquired far more treasures and wealth than he had over the years.

about the animal, reminding her of how the bull had deserted her herd in favour of his because it refused to remain in the hands of a woman. As soon as Medb heard these words, all of her property lost its value for her, and she grew adamant that she would soon find a bull to equal the Bull of Finnbennach even if she had to scour the entire

countryside for it and bring it back to Connacht by force.

Mac Roth, the King's steward, was summoned to appear before Medb and when she questioned him on the whereabouts of such a bull, he was able to tell her without any hesitation exactly where the best specimen in the country might be found:

'It belongs to Daire mac Fiachna in the province of Ulster,' he told the Queen. 'It is known as the Brown Bull of Cooley and is regarded as the finest beast in the whole of Erin.'

'Then you must go to the son of Fiachna and ask him for the loan of the bull for a year,' replied Medb, 'informing him that at the end of this time, the beast will be safely returned to him, together with fifty of the finest heifers my kingdom has to offer. And if Daire chooses to bring the bull here himself, he may add to his reward a measure of land equalling the size of his present domain in Ulster and a splendid war chariot worthy of the bravest of Connacht's warriors.'

On the following morning, a group of nine foot-messengers led by mac Roth set off in the direction of Ulster, carrying with them a number of gifts from Queen Medb to the owner of the bull, including an oak chest loaded with gold and silver ornaments and several decorated bronze flagons filled with the finest mead in the land. The mere sight of such a treasure-laden party approaching the fort of Daire mac Fiachna raised the spirits of all who set eyes on them and a very warm welcome was lavished on the men. Then Daire himself came forward to greet the party and enquired of them the purpose of their journey to his home. Mac Roth began to tell him of the squabble between Medb and Ailill and of how the Queen had decided that she must quickly find a bull to match the impressive Bull of Finnbennach. Flattered that his own beast had achieved such fame in Connacht, Daire was immediately disposed to help Queen Medb as best he could, but when he heard of the generous reward he would receive in return for the loan of his property, he was well pleased with himself and gave the order at once for the Bull of Cooley to be prepared for its journey to Connacht the next day.

The evening was spent feasting and drinking and a happy atmosphere prevailed for a time as the men of the two provinces exchanged friendly conversation. But as the wine flowed, the tongues of Queen Medb's messengers began to loosen and in the company of their hosts they began to brag of their army's great strength:

'It is just as well for Daire,' boasted one of Medb's envoys, 'that he has surrendered the beast willingly to us. For if he had

Opposite: Medb grew adamant that she would soon find a bull to equal the Bull of Finnbennach even if she had to scour the entire countryside for it.

refused to do so, the Queen's mighty army would have marched on Ulster and taken the bull from him without any trouble at all.'

When Daire's men heard these offensive remarks, they went straightaway to their master's quarters and demanded that he avenge such a dreadful insult. Mac Roth was immediately summoned to appear before Daire who angrily informed him of the conversation that had been overheard.

'Go back to your Queen,' said Daire, 'and tell her that she shall never take from me by foul means what she cannot win by fair. Let Medb and Ailill invade Ulster if they dare, for we are well equipped to meet the challenge.'

Before the break of day, Medb's messengers had set off for Connacht to deliver the unhappy tidings to their Queen. But when Medb saw that they had not returned with the Brown Bull of Cooley, she did not fly into the rage they had expected. Instead, she spoke calmly to mac Roth:

'I have foreseen this result,' she told him. 'Your dispute with the son of Fiachna is of little consequence, for I have always known that if the Brown Bull of Cooley was not given willingly, he would be taken by force. That time is now arrived, and taken he shall be!'

So began the Queen of Connacht's great war on Ulster, one of the bloodiest wars the country had ever before endured. From every corner of Erin came the allies of Medb and Ailill, including Fraech, son of Fidach, and Calatin, accompanied by his twenty-seven sons. Warriors of great renown from the provinces of Leinster and Munster swelled the numbers of

Medb's armed legions, and they were joined by many heroic Ulstermen, among them Fergus mac Roy and Cormac, son of Conchobar, who had defected from their own army, unhappy with their King's leadership.

Not a day or a night passed without a fierce and fiery combat between the armies of Connacht and Ulster. Rivers and streams ran crimson with blood and the bodies of the slain littered the emerald hills and plains. Medb was not slow to display her true worth as a warrior in her own right and Fergus, her chief scout, proved himself a most loyal and courageous comrade in arms. Yet there was none among Medb's great army who could emulate the feats of one particular Ulster warrior, a youthful figure who seemed utterly invincible and who drove himself against them time and time again, bursting with renewed vitality and strength on each occasion.

Cuchulainn, leader of Ulster's Red Guard, was well known to both Fergus and Cormac, but he had grown stronger and more powerful than they had ever imagined possible during their brief time of exile. And as they observed his powers of command and his exceptional skill on the battlefield, they became increasingly alarmed and went before the Queen to warn her that she was faced with no ordinary opponent. Medb grew worried at this news and took counsel with the most prominent figures of her army. After some deliberation, it was decided that her most valiant warrior should be sent to do battle against Cuchulainn. The son of Daman, known as Ferdia, was nominated for this task, for he had been trained alongside Cuchulainn under the great woman-warrior Scathach in the Land of Shadows and had risen to become Connacht's champion warrior, a man feared and respected by all who encountered him.

Nothing had ever yet challenged the deep bond of friendship formed between Ferdia and Cuchulainn during their time together in the Land of Shadows. The love and respect the two men felt for each other had remained constant over the years, and whenever they found occasion to be together, it was not unusual for people to mistake them for brothers. When Ferdia discovered what Medb demanded of him, he was greatly disturbed, and though he was loathe to oppose the wishes of his sovereign, he immediately refused the Queen's request and dismissed her messengers. Then Medb sent her druids and men of poetry to Ferdia's tent, instructing them to recite the most savage and mocking verses in the loudest of voices for everybody to hear.

It was for the sake of his own honour that Ferdia agreed to meet with Medb and Ailill without any further delay. The King and

Opposite:
A mood of gloom and despair descended upon Ferdia, since he knew that one of the two great champion warriors of Erin would fail to return home alive.

Queen were more than delighted to receive him and Medb wasted no time reeling off the numerous rewards Ferdia could hope to receive if he would only obey her simple wish. But Ferdia showed no interest in the riches that were intended for him, so that Medb grew more and more angry and frustrated. She had little or nothing to lose by playing her one last card and with a tone of false resignation she addressed Ferdia once more:

'It must be true what Cuchulainn has said of you,' said Medb slyly. 'He said that you feared death by his hands and that you would be wise not to go against him. Perhaps it is just as well that the two of you do not meet.'

On hearing this, Ferdia could scarcely contain his anger:

'It was unjust of Cuchulainn to say such a thing,' he roared. 'He well knows that it is not cowardice, but love, that prevents me facing him. So it is settled then. Tomorrow I will go forth to his camp and raise my weapon against him.'

But even as he spoke these words, a mood of gloom and despair descended upon Ferdia and he walked out into the black night, his head bowed in sadness. His closest companions and servants were also overcome with grief to discover what it was that Ferdia was compelled to do, for each was troubled by the knowledge that one of the two great champion warriors of Erin would fail to return home alive.

Word had soon reached Cuchulainn that Medb had chosen his dearest friend to face him in combat and, as he watched Ferdia's war chariot approach, he was forced to acknowledge in his own mind that he would

much rather fall by his friend's weapon than slay Ferdia with his own. Yet, at the same time, he could not fully understand why his fosterbrother had so easily given into the wishes of Queen Medb. The betrayal he felt could not be ignored and he prepared himself to greet Ferdia with a degree of caution and reserve. As Ferdia stood down from his chariot, Cuchulainn did not rush forward to embrace him as he would have done in the past, but remained at a distance, waiting for his friend to make the first gesture of friendship.

'I wish that we could have met again in more favourable circumstances,' said Ferdia. 'With all my heart I long to embrace you, old friend.'

'I once would have trusted such words,' answered Cuchulainn, 'but I no longer place any trust in what you say when I know that you have abandoned our friendship for the sake of a treacherous queen and the rewards she no doubt promised you.'

'I see that treason has overcome our love,' replied Ferdia sadly, 'but it is just as well that you think this way. It is best not to remember our friendship, but to meet each other as true enemies of war.'

And so they began to choose the weapons they would use against each other and it was agreed that they would begin the day's fighting with small javelins. They hurled these at each other, backwards and forwards through the air with great energy and speed, but by the close of day, not one spear had pierced the shield of either champion. As nightfall approached, they called a truce, and agreed to resume combat with different weapons at dawn on the following morning.

On the second day, Cuchulainn and Ferdia took up the fight once more, remaining seated in their chariots as they cast heavy, broad-bladed spears at each other across the ford from noon until sundown. But on this day, they both suffered many wounds that stained their flesh red with blood. When they had grown weary of the battle, they again agreed to stop fighting until morning and, placing their weapons in the hands of their servants, they moved towards each other and kissed and embraced warmly in remembrance of their friendship. Their horses shared the same paddock that evening and their charioteers gathered round the same fire. Healing herbs were laid on their wounds and they both rested until daybreak.

Opposite:
Still the combat could not be resolved and the two warriors decided to part once more for the evening, their bodies torn to shreds.

As the third day of combat was about to commence and the two men stood opposite each other once more, Cuchulainn was suddenly struck by the change which seemed to have occurred overnight in his friend. Ferdia's brow was now deeply furrowed and his eyes reflected a deep, dark sadness. He no longer held himself upright

and he lurched forward wearily to meet his opponent. Filled with pity and sorrow, Cuchulainn pleaded with Ferdia to abandon the fighting, but his friend merely shook his head, insisting that he must fulfil his contract with Queen Medb and King Ailill. They proceeded to choose their weapons and armed themselves with full-length shields and hard-smiting swords. Then they began to strike each other savagely and viciously until they had each carved great wedges of flesh from the other's shoulder-blades and thighs. Still the combat could not be resolved and they decided to part once more for the evening, their bodies torn to shreds and their friendship shattered irreparably. And on this occasion, no kiss was exchanged between them, no curing herbs were exchanged, and their horses and charioteers slept in separate quarters.

As the sun was about to rise on the fourth morning, Ferdia arose and walked out alone to the ford of combat. He wore the jaded, sorrowful expression of a man who senses death close at hand and he began to arm himself with particular care and attention. He knew instinctively that the decisive day of the battle had arrived and that one of them would certainly fall before the evening had drawn to a close. Next to his skin he wore a tunic of silk, speckled with gold and over this he placed a thick leather smock. He then laid a huge, flat stone, which he had carried all the way from Africa, across his torso and covered it with a solid iron apron. On his head he placed a crested war-helmet, adorned with crystals and rubies. He carried in his left hand a massive shield with fifty bosses of bronze and in his right, he clutched his mighty battle-sword. And when at last he was satisfied that he had protected himself against injury as best he could, he remained by the ford, performing many impressive feats with his sword while he awaited the arrival of Cuchulainn.

It was decided between the two warriors on this fourth day that they should use whatever weapons they had to hand and once they had gathered these together the fighting began in earnest. So wild was their rage on that morning, so bitter and violent the clashing of their swords, even the goblins and demons of the air fled in fear. Every creature of the forest shrieked in terror and ran for cover, while the waters themselves changed course, recoiling from the horror and ruthlessness of the combat. And as the afternoon came and went, the wounds inflicted were now deeper and more savage. Each man, although staggering with exhaustion, sought to outdo the other and remained watchful of just such an opportunity. Then, at last, in a moment of acute weariness, Cuchulainn lowered his heavy shield and as soon as he had done so, Ferdia thrust at him with his blade, driving it cleanly through his breast, causing the blood to flow freely down the battle-warrior's tunic. Again, Ferdia struck with his sword and this time it entered Cuchulainn's stomach so that he curled over in agony and began writhing on the earth. And knowing that he must save himself before it was too late, Cuchulainn reached for the Gae Bolg, a weapon he was resolved to use only as a last resort. Taking careful aim, he let fly the instrument with his right foot so that it passed through Ferdia's protective iron apron, through to the flat stone which it broke in three pieces and into the body of his friend filling every joint and every limb with its deadly barbs.

Cuchulainn hastened towards where his friend lay and pulled him gently to his bosom.

'Death is almost upon me,' sighed Ferdia, 'and it is a sad day for us that our friendship should come to such an end. Do not forget the love we once had, Cuchulainn.'

And as Ferdia perished in his arms, Cuchulainn wept piteously, clasping his friend's cold hand lovingly in his own. Then he lifted the body from the damp earth and carried it northwards across the ford to a place where they would not be disturbed by the approaching armies of Ulster. Daylight faded and as Cuchulainn lay down next to Ferdia he fell into a death-like swoon from which he could not be roused for a full seven days.

❋　❋　❋

THE FENIAN CYCLE
TALES OF FINN MAC CUMAILL
AND THE FIANNA

he central character of the Fenian, or Ossianic Cycle is Finn mac Cumaill[1], thought to be a real historical person who lived in Ireland some time in the third century AD. A myriad of stories now exists detailing the adventures of this distinguished warrior who rose to leadership of the Fianna and whose stronghold was situated on the Hill of Allen near Co. Kildare. The tales in this cycle generally take place in the Midlands of Ireland and describe a much later epoch when life was less turbulent and the climate of war had been replaced by a more harmonious and romantic atmosphere. The men of the Fianna were not merely military soldiers therefore, but highly accomplished hunter-fighters, often trained in the wilderness, and forced to submit to a number of rigourous tests before they were accepted into the Fianna. Alongside warrior attributes, members of the Fianna were also expected to know by heart the full poet's repertoire, numbering twelve books, and to possess the gift of poetic composition. Oisín[2], son of Finn mac Cumaill, is traditionally regarded as the greatest poet of all ancient Irish tales.

The parentage of Finn and the cause of the feud between himself and the Clan of Morna are recounted in this chapter, followed by the story of The Pursuit of Diarmuid and Gráinne which is considered to be one of the most striking and inventive tales of the cycle. The visit of Oisín to Tir na N-Óg is a much later addition to the Fenian tales, and only made a first appearance in literary form in the mid-eighteenth century.

1 Pronounced Finn mac Cool.
2 Pronounced Usheen.

The Coming of Finn mac Cumaill

MANY HUNDREDS OF YEARS after the death of Cuchulainn and the Knights of the Red Guard, the Fianna of Erin reached the height of their fame under the leadership of Finn mac Cumaill. The great warriors of the Fianna were every bit as courageous as their forerunners and each was carefully chosen for his strength and fearlessness on the battlefield. They were also powerful hunters who loved the outdoor life, and many among them possessed the gift of poetry which led to the writing of beautiful tributes to the land of their birth, with its breathtaking mountain valleys and swift-flowing, silver streams. These noble Fenian fighters were above all champion protectors of Erin and during their reign no foreign invader ever dared to set foot on her illustrious shores.

Cumall, son of Trenmor of Clan Brascna, was the father of Finn mac Cumaill and he served as one of the bravest leaders of the Fianna until the day he was slain by his rival, Goll mac Morna, at the battle of Cnucha. Following his death, the Clan of Morna took control of the Fianna and the relatives and friends of Cumall were forced into hiding in the dense forests of the midlands where they built for themselves makeshift homes and yearned for the day when their household would again be restored to power. The Clan of Morna stole from the dead leader the Treasure Bag of the Fianna, filled with strange magical instruments from the Eastern World that had the power to heal all wounds and illnesses. It was placed in the charge of Lia, a chieftain of Connacht, for it was he who had dealt Cumall the first significant wound in the battle of Cnucha.

After the defeat of her husband, Muirne, wife of Cumall, hurriedly abandoned her home and fled to the west to the woodlands of Kerry, accompanied by two of her most trusted handmaidens. For she was carrying the child of the deceased warrior and wished to bring it safely into the world, out of the reach of the bloodthirsty sons of Morna. Within the month, Muirne had given birth to a son and she gave him the name of Demna. And as she gazed upon the infant's face, she was struck by its

Opposite: 'Take him under cover of darkness to a safe retreat and do not rest until you have discovered the remotest dwelling in Erin where he may grow unharmed.'

likeness to the face of Cumall, not yet cold in his grave. Tears of sorrow and anguish flooded down her cheeks and she grasped the child fiercely to her bosom, making a solemn promise to protect him from all harm and evil until he should grow to manhood.

But it was not long before Goll mac Morna received news of the birth of Cumall's heir and he rode forth in great haste through the

forests of Erin towards Kerry, intent on destroying the infant. That evening, as she lay sleeping, Muirne had a disturbing vision of a war chariot with wheels of fire approaching her home and she arose at once and summoned her handmaidens to her.

'The sons of Morna have knowledge of our whereabouts,' she told them, 'and the child is unsafe while he remains here with me. Take him under cover of darkness to a safe retreat and do not rest until you are certain you have discovered the remotest dwelling in Erin where he may grow to adulthood unharmed and untroubled.'

The two handmaidens took the tiny bundle from Muirne's arms and set off in the piercingly cold night air towards the protection of the woods. They journeyed for fourteen days by secret paths until they reached the mountains of Slieve Bloom and here, under the shelter of the sprawling oak trees, they finally came to rest, satisfied at last that they had found a true place of sanctuary.

In the fullness of time, the boy Demna grew fair and strong and the two women who cared for him taught him how to hunt and how to spear fish and they marvelled at the speed and zealousness with which he learned to do these things. Before he had reached the age of ten, he could outrun the fastest wild deer of the forests and was so accomplished in the use of his various weapons that he could bring down a hawk with a single shot from his sling, or pin down a charging wild boar with one simple thrust of his spear. It was obvious too that he had the makings of a fine poet, for he was at one with nature and grew to love her fruits, whether listening for hours to the sound of a running brook, or gazing in awe and wonder at the delicate petals of mountain snowdrops. And his nursemaids were overjoyed with their charge and knew that Muirne would be proud of the son they had reared on her behalf, though she may never again lay eyes on the child.

One day, when Demna was in his fourteenth year and had grown more adventurous in spirit, he went out alone and journeyed deep into the mountains until he had reached the place known as Mag Life on the shores of the Liffey. Here, he came upon a chieftain's stronghold and, as he peered beyond the walls of the castle, he observed a group of young boys his own age engaged in a game of hurling. He boldly approached them and expressed his desire to join them in their sport, so they presented him with a hurley and invited him to play along. Though he was outnumbered by the rest of them and was unfamiliar with the rules of the game, Demna quickly proved that he could play as well as any of

Opposite: The great warriors of the Fianna were as courageous as their forerunners and each was carefully chosen for his strength and fearlessness.

them and managed, on every occasion, to take the ball from the best players in the field. He was invited to join the group for another game on the following day and, this time, they put one half of their number against him. But again, he had little difficulty beating them off. On the third day, the group decided to test his ability even further and all twelve of them went against him. Demna was triumphant once more and his athletic skill was much admired and applauded. After this, the boys went before their chieftain and told him the story of the youth who had bravely defeated them. The chieftain asked for the young man to be brought before him and when he laid eyes on Demna's beautiful golden hair and saw the milky whiteness of his skin, he pronounced that he should be given the name of Finn, meaning 'fair one', and it was by this name that he was always known thereafter.

At the end of three months, there was not a living person in the land who had not heard rumours of the daring feats of Finn, the golden-haired youth. And it was not long before Goll mac Morna had dispatched his horsemen throughout the countryside to track down the son of Cumall, ordering them to bring him back dead or alive. Finn's two fostermothers grew anxious that he would be found and they called Finn back home to them and advised him to leave his home in the mountains of Slieve Bloom:

'The champion warriors of the sons of Morna will arrive soon,' they told him, 'and they have been instructed to kill you if they find you here. It was Goll, son of Morna, who murdered your father Cumall. Go from us now, Finn, and keep your identity secret until you are strong enough to protect yourself, for the sons of Morna know that you are the rightful leader of the Fianna and they will stop at nothing until you are dead.'

And so Finn gathered together his belongings and set off in the direction of Loch Lein in the west where he lived for a time in the outdoors, safe from the attention of everyone. At length, however, he began to yearn for the company of other warriors and could not suppress his desire to volunteer himself in military service to the King of Bantry. Even though he did not make himself known to any of his companions, it was not long before their suspicions were aroused, for there was not a soldier more intrepid, nor a hunter more accomplished in the whole of the kingdom. The King himself was curious to learn more about the young warrior and invited him to visit the palace. The two men sat down to a game of chess and the King was greatly surprised to witness the ease

Opposite: In the fullness of time, Demna grew fair and strong and his nursemaids marvelled at the speed with which he learned to do most things.

with which the youth managed to defeat him. They decided to play on, and Finn won seven games, one after another. Then the King gave up the contest and began to question his opponent warily:

'Who are you,' he asked, 'and who are your people?'

'I am the son of a peasant of the Luagni of Tara,' replied Finn.

'I do not believe this to be the truth,' said the King, 'I am convinced that you are the son that Muirne bore to Cumall. You need not fear me if this is so and I advise you, as proof, to depart here without delay, since I do not wish you to be slain by the sons of Morna while under my poor protection .'

Then Finn realized that he had little choice but to continue his wanderings over the lonely plains of Erin. And it was always the case that whenever he came into contact with other people, his beauty and noble bearing betrayed him, so that the eyes of all were fixed upon him, and the news of his presence promptly spread throughout the region.

He journeyed onwards into Connacht, restricting himself to those areas of the wilderness where he felt certain he would not encounter another living soul. But as he was on his way one morning, he heard the unmistakable sound of a woman wailing and soon came upon her in a clearing of the woods, kneeling over the body of a dead youth.

'I have good cause to mourn in such a fashion,' said the woman looking up at Finn, 'for my only son has been struck down without mercy by the tall warrior who has just passed by here.'

'And what was your son's name who suffered this cruel, unwarranted fate?' enquired Finn.

'Glonda was his name,' replied the woman, 'and I ask you, under bond as a warrior, to avenge his death, since I know of no other who can help me.'

Without hesitating a moment longer, Finn set off in pursuit of the warrior, following the tracks through the woods until he came to the dwelling place of Lia Luachair on the outskirts of Connacht. Taking up the old woman's challenge, he drew his sword and began attacking Lia, striking him down with little effort. It was then that Finn noticed a strange bag on the floor at the older man's feet, and as he looked inside, the treasures of Cumall and the Fianna were revealed to him, and he was overcome with pride that he had unwittingly slain the man who had dealt his father the first wound at Cnucha.

It was at this time that Finn grew weary of his solitary life and began to gather around him all the young warriors of the country who had come to admire his courage and determination. And one of the first tasks he set himself was to go in search of his uncle Crimall and the rest of the Clan Brascna who were still in hiding from the sons of Morna. Accompanied by his followers, he crossed the River Shannon and marched into Connacht where he found his uncle and a number of the old Fianna lying low in the heart of the forest. Crimall stepped forwards and lovingly embraced his nephew, for it was apparent at once that the young stranger before him was the son of Cumall. Then Finn presented the old man with the Bag of Treasures and told him the story from beginning to end of how he had come

upon it and slain its custodian. And as he spoke, Crimall laid out the treasures on the ground before them and all who gazed upon them grew fresh of face and strong in body and the burden of age and sorrow was instantly lifted from their brows.

'Our time of deliverance is close at hand,' shouted Crimall joyfully, 'for it has been foretold that he who recovers the Treasure Bag of the Fianna from the hands of the enemy is the one who will lead the Clan of Brascna to victory once more. Go now Finn,' he added, 'and seek out the ancient bard known as Finnegas, since he is the one destined to prepare you for the day when you will rise to your rightful position as head of the Fianna.'

Hearing these words, Finn bade the company farewell and set off alone towards the shores of the River Boyne in the east, eager to meet with the wise old druid who had schooled his father in the ways of poetry and story-telling, whose masterful instruction was deemed essential for any man aspiring to leadership of the Fianna.

For seven long years, Finnegas had lived on the banks of the Boyne, seeking to catch the Salmon of Fec. The salmon, which swam in a deep pool overhung by hazel boughs, was famous throughout the land, for it was prophesied that the first person to eat of its flesh would enjoy all the wisdom of the world. And it happened one day that while Finn was sitting by the river with Finnegas at his side, the salmon swam boldly towards them, almost daring them to cast their rods into the water. Finnegas lost no time in doing so and was astounded when the fish got caught on his hook, struggling only very weakly to release itself. He hauled the salmon onto the shore and watched its silver body wriggle in the sand until all life had gone out of it. When it finally lay still, he gave the salmon over to Finn and ordered him to build a fire on which to cook it.

'But do not eat even the smallest morsel,' Finnegas told him, 'for it is my reward alone, having waited patiently for seven years.'

Finn placed a spit over the fire and began turning it as requested until the fish was cooked through. He then placed it on a plate and took it to Finnegas.

'And have you eaten any of the salmon?' asked the poet.

'No,' answered Finn, 'but I burned my thumb while cooking it and put it in my mouth to relieve the pain.'

'Then you are indeed Finn mac Cumaill,' said Finnegas, 'and I bear you no ill-will for having tasted the salmon, for in you the prophecy is come true.'

Opposite: 'I have good cause to mourn in such a fashion . . . for my only son has been struck down without mercy by the tall warrior who has just passed by.'

Then Finnegas gave Finn the rest of the salmon to eat and it brought him instant knowledge of all he desired to know. And that evening he composed the finest of verses, proving that he possessed a talent equal to the most gifted poets in Erin:

May-day! delightful day!
Bright colours play the vale along.
Now wakes at morning's slender ray
Wild and gay the Blackbird's song.

Now comes the bird of dusty hue,
The loud cuckoo, the summer-lover;
Branchy trees are thick with leaves;
The bitter, evil time is over.

Loaded bees with puny power
Goodly flower-harvest win;
Cattle roam with muddy flanks;
Busy ants go out and in.

Through the wild harp of the wood
Making music roars the gale—
Now it settles without motion,
On the ocean sleeps the sail.

Men grow mighty in the May,
Proud and gay the maidens grow;
Fair is every wooded height;
Fair and bright the plain below.

A bright shaft has smit the streams,
With gold gleams the water-flag;
Leaps the fish and on the hills
Ardour thrills the leaping stag.

Loudly carols the lark on high,
Small and shy his tireless lay,
Singing in wildest, merriest mood,
Delicate-hued, delightful May.[1]

---

[1] This abridged version of 'May-Day' is taken from *The High Deeds of Finn* by T.W. Rolleston.

The Rise of Finn to Leadership of the Fianna

AFTER FINN HAD EATEN of the Salmon of Fec which gave him all the gifts of wisdom, he had only to put his thumb in his mouth and whatever he wished to discover was immediately revealed to him. He knew beyond all doubt that he had been brought into the world to take the place of Cumall as head of the Fianna, and was confident at last that he had learned from Finnegas all that he would ever need to know. Turning his back on the valley of the Boyne, he set off to join Crimall and his followers in the forests of Connacht once more in order to plan in earnest for his future. He had by now become the most courageous of warriors, yet this quality was tempered by a remarkable generosity and gentleness of spirit that no man throughout the length and breath of the country could ever hope to rival. Finn was loved and admired by every last one of his comrades and they devoted their lives to him, never once slackening in their efforts to prove themselves worthy of his noble patronage.

It was decided among this loyal group that the time had come for Finn to assert his claim to the leadership of the Fianna and they went and pledged him their support and friendship in this bravest of quests. For it was well known that the Clan of Morna, who continued to rule the Fenian warriors, would not surrender their position without a bitter struggle. Finn now believed himself ready for such a confrontation and the day was chosen when he and his army would march to the Hill of Tara and plead their case before Conn Céadchathach, the High King of Erin.

As it was now the month of November and the Great Assembly of Tara was once more in progress, a period of festivity and good-will, when every man was under oath to lay aside his weapon. Chieftains, noblemen, kings and warriors all journeyed to Tara for the splendid event and old feuds were forgotten as the wine and mead flowed freely and the merry-making and dancing lasted well into the small hours. It was not long before Finn and his band of followers had arrived at Tara and they proceeded at once to the main banqueting hall where they were welcomed by the King's attendants and seated among the other Fenian warriors. As soon as he had walked into the hall, however, all eyes had been turned towards Finn, and a flurry of hushed enquiries circulated around the room as to the identity of the golden-haired youth. The King too, was quick to acknowledge that a stranger had entered his court, and he picked up a goblet of wine and instructed one of his servants to present it to the young warrior. At this gesture of friendship, Finn felt reassured in approaching the King, and he walked forward to the royal table and introduced himself to one and all.

'I am Finn, son of Cumall,' he declared, 'and I have come to take service with you, High King of Erin, just as my father did before me as head of the Fianna.'

And when he heard these words, Goll mac Morna, who sat at the King's right hand, grew pale in anger, and shuddered to hear the King respond favourably to the young warrior:

'I would be honoured to have you serve in my ranks,' replied Conn Céadchathach. 'If you are the son of Cumall, son of Trenmor, then you are also a friend of mine.'

After this, Finn bound himself in loyalty to the King, and his own band of men followed his example, and each was presented with a sword of the Fianna which they accepted with great pride and humility.

Everybody in the kingdom had either heard of Aillen the goblin or seen the creature with their own eyes. Every year during the Great Assembly, Conn Céadchathach increased the number of men guarding the royal city, but still the goblin managed to pass undetected through the outer gates, moving swiftly towards the palace and setting it alight with its flaming breath. Not even the bravest of warriors could prevent Aillen from reeking havoc on Tara, for he carried with him a magic harp and all who heard its fairy music were gently lulled to sleep. The King lived in hope however, that one day the goblin would be defeated and he adamantly refused to be held to ransom by the creature, insisting that the annual festivities take place as normal. A handsome reward awaited that warrior who could capture or destroy Aillen, but none had yet succeeded in doing so. It was at this time that Goll mac Morna conceived of his wicked plan to belittle his young rival before the King, for he could see that Conn Céadchathach secretly entertained the hope that Finn would rescue Tara from further destruction. He called the young warrior to him and told him of the one true way to win the King's favour, being careful not to mention the enchanting harp or the difficulty of the task that lay ahead:

Opposite: Every year the goblin managed to pass undetected through the outer gates, moving swiftly towards the palace and setting it alight with its flaming breath.

'Go and bind yourself before the King to rid this city of the terrible goblin who every year burns it to the ground,' said Goll. 'You alone possess the courage to do this Finn, and you may name your price if you are successful.'

So Finn went before the King and swore that he would not rest in peace until he had slain Aillen the goblin.

'And what would you have as your reward?' asked the King.

'If I manage to rid you of the goblin,' Finn replied, 'I should like to take up my rightful position as captain of the Fianna. Will you agree, under oath, to such a reward?'

'If this is what you desire,' answered the King, 'then I bind myself to deliver such a prize.'

Satisfied with these words, Finn took up his weapon and ventured out into the darkness to begin his lonely vigil over the palace.

As night fell and the November mists began to thicken round the hill of Tara, Finn waited anxiously for the goblin to appear. After some time, he saw an older warrior enter the courtyard and make his way towards him. He noticed that the warrior held in his hand a long, pointed spear, protected by a case of the soft, shining leather.

'I am Fiacha,' said the warrior gently, 'and I was proud to serve under your father, Cumall, when he was leader of the Fianna. The spear I carry is the spear of enchantment which Cumall placed in my charge upon his death.

'Take this weapon,' he added, 'and as soon as you hear the fairy music, lay its blade against your forehead and you will not fall under the melody's spell.'

Finn thanked the warrior for his gift and turned it over to inspect it, admiring its shining handle of Arabian gold and the sharp steel body of the blade that glinted challengingly in the moonlight. Then he began to roam the ramparts once more, straining his ear to catch the first notes of the magic harp. He gazed out over the wide, frosty plains of Meath but still there was no sign of the evil goblin. He had almost given up hope that Aillen would appear and had sat down wearily on the hard, frozen earth, when he caught sight of a shadowy, phantom-like figure in the distance, floating eerily over the plain towards the royal palace. At first the strange music that wafted through the air was scarcely audible, but as the goblin drew nearer, the sweet sound of the harp strings filled the air like a potent fragrance, intoxicating the senses and inducing a warm, drowsy feeling. Finn was immediately enraptured by the sound and his eyelids slowly began to droop as the music weaved its magic spell over him. But something within him struggled against the opiate of the melody and his fingers searched for the spear of enchantment. Releasing the weapon from its leather shroud, he lay

Opposite: Every year in the month of November, chieftains, noblemen, kings and warriors all journeyed to Tara for the Great Assembly.

the cold steel blade against his forehead and drew a long, deep breath as he allowed its rejuvenating strength to flow through his tired limbs.

As soon as Aillen had reached the crest of the Hill of Tara he began to spit blazing fire-balls through the palace gates, unaware that Finn had escaped the enchantment of the harp. Now Aillen had never before come face to face with an alert and animate mortal, and the sudden appearance of the young warrior quenching the flames with the cloak off his back prompted a shriek of terror and alarm. Turning swiftly around in the direction he had come from, Aillen fled for his safety, hoping to reach the fairy mound at Sliabh Fuaid before Finn could overtake him. But the young warrior was far too fleet of foot and before the goblin had managed to glide through the entrance of the mound, Finn had cast his spear, striking down the goblin with a single fatal blow through the chest. Then Finn bent over the corpse and removed Aillen's head and carried it back to the palace so that all were made aware that he had put an end to the reign of destruction.

When the sun had risen on the following morning, the King was overjoyed to discover that his kingdom remained untouched by the goblin's flame. He knew at once that Finn must have fulfilled his promise and was eager to express his gratitude. He called together all the men of the Fianna and sent his messenger to Finn's chamber requesting him to appear before him. Then the King stood Finn at his right hand and addressed his audience slowly and solemnly with the following words:

'Men of Erin,' said the King, 'I have pledged my word to this young warrior that if he should ever destroy the goblin Aillen, he would be granted leadership of the Fianna. I urge you to embrace him as your new leader and to honour him with your loyalty and service. If any among you cannot agree to do this, let him now resign his membership of the Fianna.'

And turning to face Goll mac Morna, the King asked him:

'Do you swear service to Finn mac Cumaill, or is it your decision to quit the Fianna?'

'The young warrior has risen nobly to his position,' replied Goll, 'and I now bow to his superiority and accept him as my captain.'

Then Goll mac Morna swore allegiance to Finn and each warrior came forward after him and did the same in his turn. And from this day onwards it was deemed the highest honour to serve under Finn mac Cumaill, for only the best and bravest of Erin's warriors were privileged to stand alongside the most glorious leader the Fianna had ever known.

Opposite: Every warrior in the kingdom except for Finn was gently lulled to sleep by the music from Aillen's magic harp.

The Pursuit of Diarmuid and Gráinne

FOLLOWING THE DEATH of his wife Maignes, Finn mac Cumaill had spent an unhappy year alone as a widower. The loss of his wife had come as a severe blow to the hero of the Fianna and even though he was surrounded by loved ones, including his beloved son Oisín and his grandson Oscar, who watched over and comforted him, he could not rid himself of thoughts of Maignes and was increasingly overwhelmed by deep feelings of loneliness and despair.

One morning, seeing his father in such a pitiful state of grief, Oisín called upon his most trusted friend, Diorruing O'Baoiscne, and together they agreed that something must be done to rescue Finn from his prolonged melancholy. It was Diorruing who suggested that perhaps the time had come for Finn to take a new wife and the two young men began to consider who best would fill this role. And as they pondered this question, Oisín suddenly remembered that the High King of Erin, Cormac mac Art, was said to possess one of the most beautiful daughters in the land. Her name was Gráinne, and although several suitors had sought her hand, it was known that she had not consented to marry any of them and was still in search of a husband.

Oisín and Diorruing went before Finn and expressed their concern that he had not yet recovered his good spirits. Finn listened attentively, and he could not deny that every word they spoke was the truth. But he had tried, he told them, to put aside all memory of his wife, and his attempts so far had been utterly futile.

'Will you let us help you then?' Oisín asked his father. 'For we feel certain that you would be better off with a strong woman by your side. The maiden you seek is named Gráinne, daughter of Cormac mac Art, and if you will allow it, we will journey to Tara on your behalf and request her hand in marriage.'

After they had persuaded Finn that he had little to lose by agreeing to such a venture, both Oisín and Doirruing set off for the royal residence at Tara. So impressive was their stature as warriors of the Fianna, that as soon as they arrived, they were respectfully escorted through the palace gates and permitted an immediate audience with the King. And when Cormac mac Art heard that Finn mac Cumaill desired to take his daughter for a wife, he was more than pleased at the prospect, yet at the same time, he felt it his duty to

Opposite: Gráinne, daughter of the High King of Erin, Cormac mac Art, was said to be one of the most beautiful maidens in the land.

inform Oisín of the outcome of Gráinne's previous courtships:

'My daughter is a wilful and passionate woman,' the King told Oisín. 'She has refused the hand of some of the finest princes and battle-champions Erin has ever known. Let her be brought before us so that she may give you her own decision on the matter, for I would rather not incur your displeasure by saying yes, only to have her go against me.'

So Gráinne was brought before them and the question was put to her whether or not she would have Finn mac Cumaill for a husband. And it was without the slightest show of interest or enthusiasm that Gráinne made the following reply:

'If you consider this man a fitting son-in-law for you, father, then why shouldn't he be a suitable husband for me?'

But Oisín and Doirruing were satisfied with this answer and taking their leave of the King after having promised to visit as soon as possible in the company of Finn mac Cumaill, they hastened back to the Hill of Allen to deliver the good news.

Within a week, the royal household of Tara was busy preparing itself to welcome the leader of the Fianna and the captains of the seven battalions of his great army. An elaborate banquet was prepared in their honour and King Cormac mac Art received his visitors with great pride and excitement. Then he led the way to the vast dining hall and they all sat down to enjoy a merry evening of feasting and drinking. Seated at Cormac's left hand was his wife, Eitche, and next to her sat Gráinne, resplendent in a robe of emerald silk which perfectly enhanced her breathtaking beauty. Finn mac Cumaill took pride of place at the King's right hand and beside him were seated the most prominent warriors of the Fianna according to his rank and patrimony.

After a time, Gráinne struck up a conversation with her father's druid Daire who sat close by, demanding to know of him the cause of the great celebrations taking place.

'If you are not aware of the reason,' said the druid, 'then it will indeed be hard for me to explain it to you.'

But Gráinne continued to pester Daire with the same question until eventually he was forced to give her a more direct answer:

'That warrior next to your father is none other than Finn mac Cumaill,' said the druid, 'and he has come here tonight to ask you to be his wife.'

And so, for the first time, Gráinne scrutinized the figure she had so flippantly agreed to marry, and having studied his face at some length she fell silent for a time. Then she addressed the druid once more:

'It comes as a great surprise to me,' said Gráinne, 'that it is not for his own son Oisín, or even his grandson Oscar, that Finn seeks me as a wife, since it would be far more appropriate if I married one of these two than marry this man who must be three times my own age.'

'Do not say such things,' answered Daire worriedly, 'for if Finn were to hear you, he would certainly now refuse you and none among the Fianna would ever dare to look at you afterwards.'

But Gráinne merely laughed to hear these words and her eye began to wander in the direction of the young Fenian warriors at the banqueting table. As she surveyed each of them in turn, she questioned the druid as to their identity, desiring to know what exceptional qualities they each had to recommend them. And when her eyes came to rest upon one particularly handsome warrior with dusky-black hair, her interest was very keenly aroused.

'That is Diarmuid, son of Dubne,' the druid informed her, 'who is reputed to be the best lover of women and of maidens in all the world.'

As she continued to sip her wine, Gráinne stared even more closely at the black-haired youth until eventually she called her attendant to her and whispered in her ear:

'Bring me the jewelled goblet from my chamber closet that holds enough wine for nine times nine men.' she told her. 'Have it filled to the brim with wine, then set it down before me.'

When her servant returned with the heavy goblet Gráinne added to it the contents of a small phial she had secretly hidden in a fold of her gown.

'Take the goblet to Finn first of all,' she urged her handmaiden, 'and bid him swallow a draught of wine in honour of our courtship. After he has done so, pass the goblet to all of the company at the high table, but be careful not to allow any of the youthful warriors of the Fianna to drink from it.'

The servant did as she was requested and it was not long before all who swallowed the wine from Gráinne's cup had fallen into a deep and peaceful slumber. Then Gráinne rose quietly from her place at the table and made her way towards where Diarmuid was seated.

'Will you receive my love, Diarmuid,' Gráinne asked him, 'and escape with me tonight to a place far away from here?'

'It is Finn mac Cumaill you are set to wed,' answered the young warrior, stunned at her suggestion. 'I would not do such a thing for any woman who is betrothed to the leader of the Fianna.'

'Then I place you under bonds as a warrior of the King,' said Gráinne, 'to take me out of Tara tonight and to save me from an unhappy union with an old man.'

'These are evil bonds indeed,' said Diarmuid, 'and I beg you to withdraw them, for I cannot understand what it is I have done to deserve such unwarranted punishment.'

'You have done nothing except allow me to fall in love with you,' replied Gráinne, 'ever since the day, many years ago, when you visited the palace and joined in a game of hurling on the green of Tara. I turned the light of my eyes on you that day, and I never gave my love to any other man from that time until now, nor will I ever, Diarmuid.'

Torn between his loyalty to Finn, and an allegiance to the sacred bonds Gráinne had placed him under, Diarmuid turned to his Fenian friends for counsel and advice. But all of them, including Oisín, Oscar, Diorruing and Cailte, advised that he had little choice but to go with Gráinne:

'You have not invited Gráinne's love,' Oisín told him, 'and you are not responsible for the bonds she has laid upon you. But he is a miserable wretch who does not honour his warrior's oath. You must follow Gráinne therefore, and accept this destiny, though your own death may come of it.'

Filled with despair and sorrow at these words, Diarmuid gathered up his weapons and then moving towards his comrades, he embraced each of them sadly, knowing that his days with the Fianna had now come to an end, to be replaced by days of tortured exile, when Finn mac Cumaill would ruthlessly pursue the couple from one end of Erin to the next.

As soon as the flight of Diarmuid and Gráinne had been brought to his attention, the leader of the Fianna was consumed with violent jealousy and rage and swore the bitterest revenge on the pair. At once, Finn mac Cumaill called for his horses to be saddled and a great host of his men set off on the trail of the couple, journeying for days along the most secluded tracks through the densest forests of Erin until they had crossed the river Shannon and arrived near to the place known as Doire Da Both. On the

Opposite: Diarmuid now knew that his time with Fianna had come to an end to be replaced by days of tortured exile.

outskirts of this forest, the Fenian trackers discovered a makeshift camp dusted with the ashes of a small fire, which although now cold, left them in little doubt that they were moving very closely behind their prey.

On the following evening, after they had travelled a lengthy
distance deeper into the forest, Finn and his men came upon a form of
wooden enclosure built of saplings, stones and mud, containing seven
narrow doors. Climbing to one of the tallest trees, Finn's chief scout peered
inside the structure and saw there Diarmuid and a woman lying next to him
on a blanket of deer-skin. The men of the Fianna were ordered to stand
guard at each of the seven exits and then Finn himself approached the hut
and shouted loudly for Diarmuid to come forward and surrender himself to
them. Diarmuid awoke abruptly from his sleep and taking Gráinne by the
hand thrust his head through the smallest of the doors. But his eyes
betrayed not the slightest glimmer of fear to see Finn and his great warriors
surrounding the hut. Instead, he clasped Gráinne closer to him and planted
three kisses on her lips for all the men of the Fianna to observe. Finn mac
Cumaill was seized by a fury on seeing this, and proclaimed at once that the
removal of Diarmuid's head by whatever method his men were forced to
employ would alone prove fitting reprisal for so brazen a show of disrespect.

Now Aengus Óg, the god of love, was the foster-father of
Diarmuid, son of Dubne, the deity who had protected and watched over the
couple since the night they had fled the palace of Tara. And witnessing their
plight at the hands of the Fianna, Aengus now took it upon himself to come
to their aid, drifting invisibly towards them on the breeze.

'Come and take shelter under my cloak,' he appealed to them, 'and
we will pass unseen by Finn and his people to a place of refuge and safety.'

But Diarmuid insisted that he would remain behind to face his
former comrades as a true warrior, and requested that Aengus take only
Gráinne with him. So Aengus drew Gráinne under his mantel for protection
and they both rose up into the air, gliding towards the woodlands of the
south where they felt certain Diarmuid would survive to meet up with them
later.

After he had bid Aengus and Gráinne farewell, Diarmuid stood
upright, tall and proud, and prepared himself for the task of fighting his
way through the formidable band of Fenian warriors. Taking up his weapon,
he approached the first of the seven doors and demanded to know which of
his former comrades stood behind it waiting to do combat with him:

'I wish you no harm, Diarmuid,' replied the gentle voice of Oisín.
'Let me guide you out through this door, and I promise I will not raise a
finger to hurt you.'

And on each of the other doors upon which he knocked, apart

from the very last, Diarmuid met with the same response, for it appeared that not one among his old friends of the Fianna was prepared to meet him with hostility. Finally, however, Diarmuid arrived at the seventh door and this time when he knocked, the response was anything but warm and friendly:

'It is I, Finn mac Cumaill,' came the thundering reply, 'a man who bears you no love, as you well know. And if you should come out through this gate I would take great pleasure in striking you down and cleaving asunder every last bone in your body.'

'I will not go out by any other door in that case,' answered Diarmuid, 'for I would not wish such raw anger to be unleashed on any of my friends gathered here whose desire it is to let me go free.'

And then, having driven the shafts of his mighty spears firmly into the earth, Diarmuid used them to spring high into the air, leaping over the walls of the wooden hut, clean over the heads of Finn and his men. So swift was this manoeuvre, so light his descent on the grass beyond the warrior group, that none could trace the path of his escape and they stood looking on in amazement, deliberating a long time whether or not it was some goblin of the air who had helped carry Diarmuid so effortlessly to freedom.

It was not long before Diarmuid had arrived at the clearing in the woods where Aengus and Gráinne waited anxiously to see him. Great was their relief to know that he had escaped the Fianna unharmed and they both listened in admiration as he related to them the tale of his daring escape. When the excitement of the reunion had abated however, Aengus Óg grew more serious and spoke earnestly to his foster-son and Gráinne:

'I must now depart from you,' he said to them, 'but I leave you with these words of advice. Do not slacken in caution while Finn mac Cumaill remains in pursuit of you. Never enter a cave with only one opening; and never take refuge on an island with only one harbour. Always eat your meals in a place different to where you have cooked them; never rest your head where you eat your meal, and wherever you sleep tonight, make sure you choose a fresh bed on the following night.'

For many months afterwards, Diarmuid and Gráinne followed the advice of Aengus Óg and lived precisely as he had counselled them. But the time came when they grew weary once more of shifting from place to place and they longed for even two nights together when they might sleep under the same familiar oak tree or heather bush. They had by now reached the forests of the west and had entered a bower guarded by the fierce giant Searbhán.

'Surely we may rest awhile here, Diarmuid,' said Gráinne. 'Is it not the most unlikely thing in the world that Finn and his men would find us out in such a lonely and shaded part of the woods?'

And seeing the look of exhaustion on Gráinne's face, Diarmuid agreed to go in search of Searbhán to beg permission to shelter in the forest. The giant also took pity on Gráinne and it was soon settled that the couple were free to roam the forests and hunt for their food for up to three days provided neither of them touched the quicken tree of Dubros growing in its centre or ate any of its sweet-smelling berries. For this particular tree belonged to the people of the Fairymounds who did not wish that any mortal should eat of its fruit and share the gift of immortality. And so Diarmuid accepted responsibility for both himself and Gráinne and swore upon his sword that during their short stay the berries would remain the sacred property of the fairies.

As for Finn mac Cumaill and his loyal followers of the Fianna, they had not tired in their quest for revenge and were little more than half a day's journey away from the outskirts of Searbhán's forest. And it was while Finn awaited news from his scouts, sent forth to search for evidence of Diarmuid and Gráinne, that he observed a group of horsemen approaching the Fenian camp. He recognized these riders at once as the offspring of the sons of Morna who had murdered his father at the battle of Cnucha and with whom he still had a long-standing feud. But it soon became apparent that these young warriors had travelled a great distance to beg forgiveness for the sins of their fathers and to be reconciled to the Fianna.

Now when Finn's scouts returned to inform him that Diarmuid and Gráinne rested under the protection of Searbhán beneath the tree of Dubros, Finn made up his mind to test the commitment of the warriors of the Clan of Morna:

'If you truly seek forgiveness,' he told them, 'go forth into the woods and bring me one of two things, either the head of Diarmuid, son of Dubne, or a fistful of berries from the tree of Dubros.'

And when the offspring of Morna heard this request, they answered the leader of the Fianna innocently:

Opposite:
During their time in the wilderness, the couple were watched over by one of the Danann gods, Aengus Óg, the guardian of all would-be lovers.

'We would be honoured to perform such a task. Point us in the direction of the woods and we shall soon return with one of these two prizes.'

When they were still quite a long way off however, Diarmuid spotted the warriors of Clan Morna approaching and he made ready

his weapon for attack. And as they came closer he jumped to the earth from a tree above, blocking the path of their progress.

'Who are you,' Diarmuid asked them, 'and why have you come to the forest of Searbhán?'

'We are of the Clan of Morna,' they replied, 'and we have been sent here by Finn mac Cumaill to perform one of two tasks, either to recover the head of Diarmuid, son of Dubne, or to escape here with a fistful of berries from the tree of Dubros.'

'I am the man whose head you seek,' replied Diarmuid, 'and over there is the tree bearing the fruit you are required to remove. But it will be no easy task for you to accomplish either of these things. Choose now which of the two feats you would attempt to perform.'

'I would sooner fight for your head,' answered the eldest of the warriors, 'than go against the giant Searbhán.'

So the children of Morna began wrestling with Diarmuid who had little or no difficulty overcoming them and within minutes they had been bound hand and foot by him.

Then Gráinne, who had been watching the struggle with some amusement, came forward and began to question Diarmuid about the berries. And when she heard of their magic properties, and of how, in particular, they could make the old young and beautiful once more, she insisted that she must taste them before putting any other food in her mouth again. It was useless for Diarmuid to try and persuade her otherwise, and he began to sharpen his spear, resigned to the fact that he must soon confront the tree's ferocious guardian. Seeing that he was reluctant to break his bond of friendship with the giant, the children of Morna offered to go and get the berries for Gráinne. But although Diarmuid would not agree to this, he was nonetheless touched by their generosity and offered to loosen their bonds so that they might witness the combat.

And so Diarmuid, accompanied by the children of Morna, went forward and roused the giant from his sleep, demanding that he hand over some of the precious berries for Gráinne to eat. Furious at this request, the giant swung his mighty club over his shoulder and brought it down hard in Diarmuid's direction. But Diarmuid managed to leap aside, avoiding any injury, and then hurled himself at the giant forcing him to loosen his hold on the club so that it fell heavily to the ground. Seizing the weapon, Diarmuid delivered three strong blows to the giant's head, dashing his brains to pieces. And when he was certain that Searbhán was dead, he climbed the tree of Dubros and plucked the juiciest berries, handing one bunch to Gráinne and the other to the children of Morna.

'Take these berries to Finn,' he told the warriors, 'and do not pretend to him that you have seen me. Tell him instead that you have earned his forgiveness by slaying the giant with your own bare hands.'

The children of Morna were more than happy to do this, and they expressed their gratitude to Diarmuid that he had finally brought peace between the two clans. And having placed the berries carefully in their saddlebags, they made their way back towards Finn and the men of the Fianna.

As soon as he laid eyes on the berries, Finn mac Cumaill placed them under his nose and announced at once that it was Diarmuid, not the offspring of Morna, who had gathered them:

'For I can smell his skin on them,' roared Finn, 'and I will now go myself in search of him and remove his head with my own sword.'

And he tore through the forest as fast as his horse could carry him until he reached the tree of Dubros where he suspected Diarmuid and Gráinne must be hiding. Here he sat down and called for Oisín to bring his chess-board to him. The two began to play a long and complicated game, for they were each as skilled as the other, until eventually they reached a point where the victor of the game would be decided by Oisín's next move. And Diarmuid, who had been closely following the game from above, could not prevent himself from helping his friend. Impulsively, he threw a berry down from one of the branches where it landed on the board indicating to Oisín how the game should be won. At this, Finn rose rapidly to his feet and calling all the warriors of the Fianna together he ordered them to surround the tree. Then Garb of Sliab Cua announced that Diarmuid had slain his father and that nothing would make him happier than to avenge this death. So Finn agreed to this and Garb climbed the tree in pursuit of Diarmuid.

Again, however, Aengus Óg was watchful of his foster-son and rushed to his aid without the Fianna's knowledge. And as Diarmuid flung Garb backwards from the branches with one swift movement of his foot, Aengus put the form of his foster-son upon him so that his own warriors took off his head believing him to be Diarmuid, son of Dubne. After they had done this, Garb was again changed back into his own shape causing great distress to all who witnessed the transformation. And of the nine Fenian warriors Finn mac Cumaill ordered to ascend the tree in search of

Diarmuid, the same fate befell each of them so that Finn fell into a heavy mood of anguish and grief. And when Diarmuid announced that he would descend the tree and slaughter every living person under Finn's protection, Finn at last could tolerate the killing no longer and begged for it to come to an end.

So Diarmuid and Aengus Óg appeared before Finn and it was agreed among the three of them that peace should be restored between Finn and Diarmuid. Then the leader of the Fianna and five of his captains went to the stronghold of the High King of Erin to secure a pardon for Diarmuid and Gráinne. Once this had been done, the couple were allowed to return to their native country of west Kerry where they built for themselves a fine home and lived in peace and harmony together for a great many years to follow.

Oisín in Tír na N-Óg
The Land of Youth

FINN MAC CUMAILL, the mightiest warrior of the Fianna, had no equal among mortal men and his reputation as one of the fiercest fighters in Ireland spread with each glorious victory on the battlefield. His young son, Oisín, was a particular favourite with him, for the boy showed signs of remarkable courage at an early age and had clearly inherited his father's voracious thirst for adventure. Each time Finn gazed at his golden-haired son a memory of Blaí, the boy's mother, stirred within his breast, filling him with both joy and sorrow. Blaí was now lost to him, but the child she had borne him possessed her great beauty and gift of poetry. Oisín was a true warrior and the greatest of Fenian poets. Many women had fallen in love with him, but none had yet succeeded in winning his heart. The son of Finn mac Cumaill was happiest fighting alongside his father, or roaming the dense forests that chimed with birdsong in the company of his trusty hounds.

While hunting in the middle of the woods one summer's morning, just as the silver veil of mist was rising from the shores of Loch Lein, Oisín was struck by the most enchanting vision. A young maiden appeared before him, seated majestically on a milk-white steed. Oisín had never seen her kind before, but felt certain she must have come from the fairy world. Her luxuriant golden hair,

Opposite:
'I would be honoured to take you as my bride' Oisin spoke to Niamh 'and will be happy to depart this land of mortals.'

✣ 118 ✣

adorned by an elaborate jewelled crown, cascaded over her shoulders and she was clothed in a mantle of the finest red silk. Her saddle was made of purple and gold and her horse's hooves were placed in four shoes of gold, studded with the most precious gems. She moved gracefully towards Oisín, who was immediately entranced by her radiance and perfection. The maiden's cheeks were as delicate as the satin petals of a rose; her eyes were as bright and pure as two drops of dew on a violet; her skin was as white and delicate as the first snows of winter.

'I am Niamh[1] daughter of the great King who rules the Land of Youth,' she spoke softly. 'Your name is well known to me, brave Oisín, son of the noble Finn mac Cumaill. I have hastened here for love's sake, to woo you.'

Oisín stood bewitched before the maiden as she began to sing to him of Tír na N-Óg, the Land of Youth. Her music drifted lightly towards him like a perfumed summer breeze, and it was the sweetest sound the young warrior had ever heard.

[1] Pronounced Niav.

Delightful land of honey and wine
Beyond what seems to thee most fair –
Rich fruits abound the bright year round
And flowers are found of hues most rare.

Unfailing there the honey and wine
And draughts divine of mead there be,
No ache nor ailing night or day –
Death or decay thou ne'er shalt see!

A hundred swords of steel refined,
A hundred cloaks of kind full rare,
A hundred steeds of proudest breed,
A hundred hounds – thy meed when there!

The royal crown of the King of Youth
Shall shine in sooth on thy brow most fair,
All brilliant with gems of luster bright
Whose worth aright none might declare.

All things I've named thou shalt enjoy
And none shall cloy – to endless life –
Beauty and strength and power thou'lt see
And I'll e'er be thy own true wife! [2]

'Niamh of the Golden Hair,' Oisín spoke to her. 'I have never before met a maiden so pleasing to the eye and I long to visit the kingdom of which you sing. I would be honoured to take you as my bride and will depart this land of mortals without delay to be with you.'

Before reaching up to grasp her hand, he looked around him only once, catching a final glimpse of his father's great palace and the beautiful woodlands he had now chosen to leave behind. Bidding a valiant farewell in his heart to the men of the Fianna, he mounted the powerful horse which carried them both away towards the cliffs of the west, and further on into the crashing waves.

For five days and five nights they rode, crossing the great plains of Erin and journeying on through various kingdoms of the Otherworld. The deep sea opened up to greet them and they passed underneath the bed of the ocean into a land of golden light. Regal citadels, surrounded by luscious green lawns and exotic, vibrantly

Opposite:
'I can see you possess the blood of such mighty ancestors,' said one of the men. 'Can you lend us your strength to shift the stone?'

[2] The verses Niamh sings to Oisín of the Land of Youth were written by the poet Michael Comyn.

coloured blooms, gleamed in the rays of sparkling sunshine. A youthful knight, clad in a magnificent raiment of purple and silver, suddenly appeared alongside them, riding a white mare. A fair young maiden sat next to him on the saddle holding a golden apple in the palm of her hand. Niamh again told Oisín of the beauty of Tír na N-Óg, a land even more beautiful than the splendid images now before them. They journeyed onwards, passing from this luminous world through a raging, violent tempest, moving as swiftly as the howling winds and driving rains would carry them across mountains, valleys and bottomless dark lakes until the bright orb of the sun emerged in all its splendour once more.

The kingdom now before them was far more breathtaking than Oisín had ever imagined possible. A silver-pebbled stream wound its way towards a gently undulating hill dotted with purple and yellow orchids which breathed a rich, opulent fragrance into the air. A magnificent castle stood on the hilltop, shaded by giant leafy trees laden with ripe golden pears. The sound of honey-bees buzzing from flower to flower united melodiously with the singing of birds, languidly pruning their feathers in the amber glow of early twilight. A large crowd moved forward to welcome the couple. Minstrels played soothing, magical airs and delicate blossoms were strewn at their feet creating a soft carpet for them to tread on. The happy pair were escorted to the palace where the King and Queen had prepared a large wedding banquet. The King warmly embraced his new son-in-law and ordered the seven days of feasting and celebrations to commence.

As each new day dawned in the Land of Youth it brought with it an abundance of joy for Oisín and Niamh. Time stood absolutely still in this perfect world and they had only to wish for something and it would instantly appear. Before long, the couple were blessed with three healthy children: two handsome sons, and a beautiful daughter. The son of Finn mac Cumaill had won the admiration and respect of every person in the kingdom and he enthralled each and every subject with tales of his Fenian friends and the splendid adventures they had survived together. Only one thing now threatened to destroy his happiness. At night, Oisín was tormented by dreams of Erin and of his people, the Fianna. These dreams became more and more powerful with the passing of time and he ached with the desire to visit his homeland once again. Such a dreadful anxiety could not be hidden from Niamh, for she knew what troubled her husband and could not bear to see him suffer this deep sadness and unrest.

'Go, Oisín,' she told him, 'though it breaks my heart, I will not hinder you. But you must promise me, in the name of our love for each other and for our children, that you will not dismount on Erin's soil, for time has autonomy in the land of Erin. Hear my warning that if you touch the earth, you will never again return to the Land of Youth.'

Having listened carefully to these words of caution, Oisín rode away, guided by his magical steed across the plains leading back to his beloved country. After five long days, he arrived in his native land and made his way to the home of his father. Cheered by memories of his youth and the joyous welcome home he knew he would soon receive, he rode to the far side of the forest and waited anxiously for the thick mist to clear so that the great house would be revealed in all its regal splendour. Yet when the drizzling clouds finally dispersed, Oisín was shocked to discover only a pile of crumbling stones where the stronghold of Finn mac Cumaill had once stood firm. Utterly distressed and bewildered, he turned his horse swiftly around and galloped away in search of any mortal creature who might bring him news of the Fianna.

After what seemed an eternity, he spotted on the horizon a strange band of men toiling and sweating in their efforts to lift a slab of granite from the ground. Oisín marvelled at their small frames and their lack of strength in lifting such a trifling load.

'I am searching for the dwelling place of Finn mac Cumaill and the Fianna,' he shouted to the men.

'We have often heard of Finn,' replied a stooped, wizened figure, the eldest of the group. 'But it has been many hundreds of years since the great battle of Gabra where he and the last of the Fianna lost their lives.'

'I can see you possess the blood of such mighty ancestors,' added another of the band. 'Can you lend us your strength to shift this stone?'

Niamh's words of counsel to Oisín had not been forgotten, but he was angered by these men of Erin who stood before him so weak and feeble. Filled with a great pride in his own strength and ability, he bent forward from his horse to assist in the lifting of the slab. But the angle at which he had leaned towards the men, added to the weight of the stone, caused the animal's saddle-girth to snap and Oisín could not save himself from falling to the ground. In an instant, his steed had disappeared into thin air, his royal garments had turned to grimy sackcloth and his youthful warrior's face had become creased and lined as the burden of three hundred years of mortal life fell on him. Withered and blind, he reached out with his bony arms, grasping in the dark for some form of comfort. A wretched, pitiful cry escaped his lips and he heard again Niamh's parting words to him. As he lay helpless on the cold, damp earth, he began to weep inconsolably for the wife and children to whom he could never now return in the Land of Eternal Youth.

GLOSSARY

Aengus Óg Son of Dagda and Boann (a woman said to have given the Boyne river its name), Aengus is the Irish god of love whose stronghold is reputed to have been at New Grange. The famous tale Dream of Aengus tells of how he fell in love with a maiden he had dreamt of. He eventually discovered that she was to be found at the Lake of the Dragon's Mouth in Co. Tipperary, but that she lived every alternate year in the form of a swan. Aengus pursues the woman of his dreams and plunges into the lake transforming himself also into the shape of a swan. Then the two fly back together to his palace on the Boyne where they live out their days as guardians of would-be lovers.

Balor The evil, one-eyed King of the Fomorians and also grandfather of Lugh of the Long Arm. It was prophesied that Balor would one day be slain by his own grandson so he locked his daughter away on a remote island where he intended that she would never fall pregnant. But Cian, father of Lugh, managed to reach the island disguised as a woman, and Balor's daughter eventually bore him a child. During the second battle of Mag Tured (or Moytura), Balor was killed by Lugh who slung a stone into his giant eye.

Dagda One of the principal gods of the Tuatha De Danann, the father and chief, the Celtic equivalent of Zeus. He was the god reputed to have led the People of Dana in their successful conquest of the Fir Bolg.

Dana Also known as Danu, a goddess worshipped from antiquity by the Celts and considered to be the ancestor of the Tuatha De Danann.

Daoine Sidhe The people of the Hollow Hills, or Otherworld.

Druid An ancient order of Celtic priests held in high esteem who flourished in the pre-Christian era. The word druid is derived from an ancient Celtic one meaning 'very knowledgeable'. These individuals were believed to have mystical powers and in ancient Irish literature possess the ability to conjure up magical charms, to create tempests, to curse and debilitate their enemies and to perform as soothsayers to the royal courts.

Dun A stronghold or royal abode surrounded by an earthen wall.

Emain Macha The capital of ancient Ulster.

Fianna/Fenians The word 'fianna' was used in early times to describe young warrior-hunters. These youths evolved under the leadership of Finn mac Cumaill as a highly skilled band of military men who took up service with various kings throughout Ireland.

Fir Bolg One of the ancient, pre-Gaelic peoples of Ireland who were reputed to have worshipped the god Bulga, meaning god of lighting. They are thought to have colonized Ireland around 1970 BC, after the death of Nemed and to have reigned for a short period of thirty seven years before their defeat by the Tuatha De Danann.

Fomorians A race of monstrous beings, popularly conceived as sea-pirates with some supernatural characteristics who opposed the earliest settlers in Ireland, including the Nemedians and the Tuatha De Danann.

Gae Bolg Cuchulainn alone learned the use of this weapon from the woman-warrior, Scathach and with it he slew his own son Connla and his closest friend, Ferdia. Gae Bolg translates as 'harpoon like javelin' and the deadly weapon was reported to have been created by Bulga, the god of lighting.

Hurley A traditional Irish game played with sticks and balls, quite similar to hockey.

Macha There are thought to be several different Machas who appear in quite a number of ancient Irish stories. For the purposes of this book, however, the Macha referred to is the wife of Crunnchu. The story unfolds that after her husband had boasted of her great athletic ability to the King, she was subsequently forced to run against his horses in spite of the fact that she was heavily pregnant. Macha died giving birth to her twin babies and with her dying breath she cursed Ulster for nine generations, proclaiming that it would suffer the weakness of a woman in childbirth in times of great stress. This curse had its most disastrous effect when Medb of Connacht invaded Ulster with her great army.

Mag Muirthemne Cuchulainn's inheritance. A plain extending from River Boyne to the mountain range of Cualgne, close to Emain Macha in Ulster.

Milesians A group of iron-age invaders led by the sons of Mil, who arrived in Ireland from Spain around 500 BC and overcame the Tuatha De Danann.

Moytura Translated as the 'Plain of Weeping', Mag Tured, or Moytura was where the Tuatha De Danann fought two of their most significant battles.

Nuada The first king of the Tuatha De Danann in Ireland, who lost an arm in the first battle of Moytura against the Fomorians. He became known as 'Nuada of the Silver Hand' when Diancecht, the great physician of the Tuatha De Danann, replaced his hand with a silver one after the battle.

Ogham One of the earliest known forms of Irish writing, originally used to inscribe upright pillar stones.

Otherworld The world of deities and spirits, also known as the Land of Promise, or the Land of Eternal Youth, a place of everlasting life where all earthly dreams come to be fulfilled.

Tailtiu One of the most famous royal residences of ancient Ireland.

Tara Also known as Temair, the Hill of Tara was the popular seat of the ancient High-Kings of Ireland from the earliest times to the sixth century. Located in Co. Meath, it was also the place where great noblemen and chieftains congregated during wartime, or for significant events.

Uisneach A hill formation between Mullingar and Athlone said to mark the centre of Ireland.

General Rules on the Pronunciation of Irish

Stress usually falls on the first syllable
A stroke over a letter signifies length
Vowels are pronounced as in German or French.
For example:

A a, ai–rather; á, ái–saw; aí–aisle
E e, ei–met
I i–tin; í, íu–seen
O o–not; ó–home; óe, oí–oil
U u, ui–put; ú, úi–noon; úa, úai–moor

Consonants and consonant clusters are nearly always pronounced as in English. Some exceptions include:

c, always pronounced like a k
g, always as in girl, never as in gin
ch, always guttural, as in loch
gh, always silent

The following is an alphabetical guide to the pronunciation of key Irish words and place names used in the text as they would sound in English:

Aeb	aev
Ailill	al-il
Aoife	ee-fah
Bodb	bov
Bricriu	brik-roo
Cian	kee-un
Conchobar mac Nessa	kunna-khoor mok nassa
Conn Céadchathach	kun kaid-kho-huk
Cuchulainn	koo khul-inn
Danu	don-u
Dearg	darr-ug
Diarmuid	dee-ur-mwid
Eochaid	ukh-ee
Fianna	fee-anah
Finn mac Cumaill	finn mac cool
Fir Bolg	fir bull-ug
Gráinne	graw-nya
Lugh	lu, loo
Macha	mokk-uh
Midhir	mee-er
Ogham	oam
Oisín	ush-een
Tuatha De Danann	too-a-huh dai don-un

Suggested Further Reading

Murphy, Gerald, *Saga and Myth in Ancient Ireland*, Dublin, 1961 ● O' Hogain, Dr. Daithi, *Myth, Legend and Romance: An Encyclopaedia of the Irish Folk Tradition*, London, 1990 ● O'Rahilly, Thomas F., *Early Irish History and Mythology*, Dublin, 1946 ● O' Sullivan, S., *Legends from Ireland*, London, 1977 ● Rolleston, T.W., *Celtic Myths and Legends*, London, 1994 ● Sutcliff, F., *The High Deeds of Finn mac Cool*, London, 1967 ● Yeats, W.B., *Fairy and Folk Tales of Ireland*, Dublin, 1973

Translations

Cross, Tom P. and Slover, Clark, H., *Ancient Irish Tales*, New York, 1936 ● Kinsella, Thomas, *The Táin*, Dublin, 1969 ● Macalister, R.A.S., *Lebor Gabála Érenn, (The Book of Invasions)*, Dublin, 1938 O' Rahilly, Cecille, *Táin Bó Cúalnge from the Book of Leinster (The Cattle Raid of Cúailnge)*, Dublin, 1967

General Texts on Ireland and the Celts

Chadwick, Nora, *The Celts*, London, 1970 ● Jackson, Kenneth H., *A Celtic Miscellany*, London, 1951 ● Joyce, P.W., *A Concise History of Ireland*, Dublin, 1900 ● Mac Cana, Proinsias, *Celtic Mythology*, London, 1970 ● Raftery, Joseph, *Prehistoric Ireland*, London, 1951

Notes on Illustrations

Page 3 *Lancelot at the Chapel of the Grail* by H.J.Ford. Courtesy of The Charles Walker Collection at Images. **Page 5** *The Irish Whisky Still* by Sir David Wilkie (National Gallery of Scotland, Edinburgh). Courtesy of The Bridgeman Art Library. **Page 7** *'Celtic Deities'* by Gordon Wain (Private Collection). Courtesy of The Charles Walker Collection at Images. **Page 9** *From 'A Book of Old Ballads'* by H.M.Brock. Courtesy of The Charles Walker Collection at Images. **Page 13** *Ogam Stone from 'Celtic Deities'* by Gordon Wain (Private Collection). Courtesy of The Charles Walker Collection at Images. **Page 15** *'The Fomors'* by John Duncan (City of Dundee District Council). Courtesy of McManus Galleries, Dundee. **Page 17** *The Princess Burns the Elfrite to Death* by Edmund Dulac (Victoria & Albert Museum, London). Courtesy of the Bridgeman Art Library. **Page 18** *Druid Priest* by Gordon Wain (Private Collection). Courtesy of The Charles Walker Collection at Images. **Page 21** *Fairy and Sprites in the Undergrowth* by Georges Picard (Private Collection). Courtesy of The Bridgeman Art Library. **Page 25** The Return of Ulysses by John Linnell (Forbes Magazine Collection, New York). Courtesy of the Bridgeman Art Library. **Page 27** *Dunluce Castle, Co. Antrim* by Augustus Earl (National Library of Australia, Canberra). Courtesy of The Bridgeman Art Library. **Page 29** *Dunluce Castle, Co. Antrim* by Charles Bentley (Victoria & Albert Museum, London). Courtesy of The Bridgeman Art Library. **Page 31** *What the Little Girl Saw in the Bush* by Frederick McCubbin (Private Collection). Courtesy of The Bridgeman Art Library. **Page 35** *King Midas* by Nicolas Tournier (Phillips, The International Fine Art Auctioneers, London). Courtesy of the Bridgeman Art Library. **Page 37** *'The Children of Lir'* by John Duncan (City of Dundee District Council). Courtesy of McManus Galleries, Dundee. **Page 38** *The Daughters of Albion* by William Blake (Victoria & Albert Museum, London). Courtesy of The Bridgeman Art Library. **Page 41** *A Young Maiden* by J R Herbert (Bonhams, London). Courtesy of The Bridgeman Art Library. **Page 47** *Meditation* by William C T Dobson (Fine-Lines, Warwickshire). Courtesy of The Bridgeman Art Library. **Page 49** *Hero Awaiting the Return of Leander* by Evelyn de Morgan (Roy Miles Gallery, London). Courtesy of The Bridgeman Art Library. **Page 53** *Oberon Costume Design* by C.Wilhelm (Victoria & Albert Museum, London). Courtesy of The Bridgeman Art Library. **Page 57** *The Fire King Appears to Count Albert* by Henry Fuseli (Victoria & Albert). Courtesy of The Bridgeman Art Library. **Page 59** *Arthur in the Gruesome Glen* by Henry Clarence Whaite (Forbes Magazine Collection, London). Courtesy of the Bridgeman Art Library. **Page 61** *La Ghirlandaia* by Dante Gabriel Rossetti (Guildhall Art Gallery, London). Courtesy of The Bridgeman Art Library. **Page 63** *Slaying the Chimaera* by Giovanni-Battista Tiepolo (Palazzo Sandi-Porto, Venice). Courtesy of The Bridgeman Art Library. **Page 65** *Clearing in the Forest* by Caspar-David Friedrich (Neue Galerie, Linz). Courtesy of The Bridgeman Art Library. **Page 69** *Fallen Angels Entering Pandemonium* by John Martin (Tate Gallery, London). Courtesy of The Bridgeman Art Library. **Page 71** *Lady Macbeth* by George Cattermole (Victoria & Albert Museum, London). Courtesy of the Bridgeman Art Library. **Page 72** *Meg Merrilies* by Heywood Hardy (Roy Miles Gallery, London). Courtesy of the Bridgeman Art Library. **Page 75** *Bacchante* by Frederic Leighton (Forbes Magazine Collection, New York). Courtesy of The Bridgeman Art Library. **Page 77** *Fairy Wood* by John Hassell (Usher Gallery, Lincoln). Courtesy of The Bridgeman Art Library. **Page 79** *Macbeth Instructing the Murderers Employed to Kill Banquo* by George Cattermole (Victoria & Albert, London). Courtesy of The Bridgeman Art Library. **Page 81** *Tholla Bhriste, Connemara* by James Humbert Craig (Crawford Municipal Art Gallery, Cork). Courtesy of The Charles Walker Collection at Images. **Page 83** *The Faithful Knight* by Thomas Jones Barker (Sheffield City Art Galleries). Courtesy of The Bridgeman Art Library. **Page 85** *Sir Galahad* by Arthur Hughes (Walker Art Library, Liverpool). Courtesy of The Bridgeman Art Library. **Page 89** *The Dream of Ossian* by Jean Auguste Ingres (Musee Ingres, Montauban). Courtesy of Giraudon and The Bridgeman Art Library. **Page 91** *Ossian's Complaint* by Karoly Kisfaludy (Magyar Nemseti Galeria, Budapest). Courtesy of The Bridgeman Art Library. **Page 92** *Phedra and Hippolyte* by Baron Pierre-Narcisse (Louvre, Paris). Courtesy of Lauros-Giraudon and the Bridgeman Art Library. **Page 95** *'We will, fair queen, up to the mountain's top'* by Arthur Rackham. Courtesy of The Charles Walker Collection at Images. **Page 96** *After the Battle Between Prince Igor Sviatoslavitch of Kiev and the Polovtsi* by Viktor Vasnetsov (Tretyakov Gallery, Moscow). Courtesy of Novosti and The Bridgeman Art Library. **Page 101** *Scene from the Tempest* by William Hogarth (Nostell Priory, Yorkshire). Courtesy of the Bridgeman Art Library. **Page 103** *The Riders of the Sidhe* by John Duncan (Dundee Art Galleries and Museums). Courtesy of Dundee Art Galleries and Museums. **Page 104** *The Prince Enters the Briar Wood* by Sir Edward Burne-Jones (Faringdon Collection, Buscot, Oxon). Courtesy of The Bridgeman Art Library. **Page 107** *Venus Verticordia* by Dante Gabriel Rossetti (Russell Cotes Art Gallery & Museum, Bournemouth). Courtesy of The Bridgeman Art Library. **Page 111** *Pygmalion Covering Her eyes at the Sight of his Creation* by Helen Stratton. Courtesy of The Charles Walker Collection at Images. **Page 115** *Ossian Conjures up the Spirits on the Banks of the River Lorca* by Francois Pascal Simon Gerard (Chateau de Malmaison, Paris). Courtesy of Lauros-Giraudon and The Bridgeman Art Library. **Page 119** *Lancelot carrying off Guinevere* by H.J.Ford. Courtesy of The Charles Walker Collection at Images. **Page 121** *MacBeth and the Witches* by Henry Fuseli (National Trust, Petworth House, Sussex). Courtesy of The Bridgeman Art Library. **Page 124** *The Clown & Lear* by Albert W.Holden. Courtesy of The Charles Walker Collection at Images.

Index